At Issue

The Role of Science in Public Policy

Other Books in the At Issue Series

At Issue

The Role of Science in Public Policy

Eamon Doyle, Book Editor

GREENHAVEN
PUBLISHING

Published in 2019 by Greenhaven Publishing, LLC
353 3rd Avenue, Suite 255, New York, NY 10010

Articles in Greenhaven Publishing anthologies are often edited for length to meet page
requirements. In addition, original titles of these works are changed to clearly present
the main thesis and to explicitly indicate the author's opinion. Every effort is made to
ensure that Greenhaven Publishing accurately reflects the original intent of the authors.
Every effort has been made to trace the owners of the copyrighted material.

Cover image: Alex Wong/Getty Images

Cataloging-in-Publication Data

Names: Doyle, Eamon, editor.
Title: The role of science in public policy / edited by Eamon Doyle.
Description: New York : Greenhaven Publishing, 2019. | Series: At issue | Includes
  bibliographical references and index. | Audience: Grades 9-12.
Identifiers: LCCN ISBN 9781534503342 (library bound) | ISBN 9781534503359 (pbk.)
Subjects: LCSH: Science--Social aspects--Juvenile literature. | United States--Politics and
  government--Juvenile literature. | Policy sciences--Juvenile literature.
Classification: LCC Q180.2 R654 2019 | DDC 306.4/5/0973--dc23

Manufactured in the United States of America

Website: http://greenhavenpublishing.com

Contents

Introduction

E ven though both reflect the Enlightenment ideal of allowing reason to guide human affairs, science and public policy are often considered to occupy separate spheres of life. Science involves the rigorous development of practical reasoning and theory. It deals in numbers, measurements, and hard, concrete facts that lead to explanations about why the physical world behaves the way that it does. Politics, government, and public policy, on the other hand, have to do with moral reasoning and other primarily social modes of thinking and communicating. This is the part of life where we get together to decide issues of fairness and social organization. The institutions are also different—science happens in labs and factories, while public policy unfolds in the media and in the halls of government.

Despite the fundamental differences between these respective areas of discourse, a huge number of public issues call for dialogue between the two spheres. Environmental issues in general tend to provide one of the clearest examples of this kind of interaction.

But the interaction is much broader than public awareness. When policymakers are faced with a public health issue like excessive air pollution or water contamination, they rely on the professional and academic scientific community to provide guidance as to the viability of regulatory options. This is because politicians and staff members at regulatory agencies often do not have the necessary scientific background to determine (1) the technical nature of the problem and (2) whether or to what degree a specific intervention will be effective toward remedying the problem.

The relationship between science and public life extends well beyond environmental policy and regulation. Consider the importance of technical forensic evidence like DNA in criminal court proceedings: without scientists to act as expert witnesses, there would be no way to establish or deal with challenges to the viability of that evidence. Consider appropriations for Medicare and

Medicaid, which rely on guidance from doctors, pharmacologists, and other researchers about the relative effectiveness of various treatments. As long as human affairs are based in the material world, science will have a role to play in many areas of public policy.

The overlap between science and public policy can be messy and controversial, particularly where commercial interests are involved. For example, companies in the manufacturing and energy sectors are often wary of environmental regulation because they generally have the most to lose when penalties or standards are imposed on emissions and other environmental impacts of commercial activity. Health and product safety issues can produce similar tensions. For instance, throughout the second half of the twentieth century, tobacco companies used a variety of legal and public relations tactics to fight public awareness of the health effects of smoking and guard themselves against potential penalties or regulations.[1]

Other examples of controversy have more to do with cultural and ideological forces. And still others involve a complicated relationship between the commercial interests, cultural forces, and structural systems in contemporary electoral politics. The prototypical example of this complex, multi-layered interaction between science, politics, and public policy is the controversy over global climate change, which has come to represent not only the intersection between science and public policy but also the divide between liberals and conservatives in America.

In presenting the issue of climate change to the public, scientists face fierce opposition. Oil companies, conservative scientists, and free market libertarians fight together and rally against a scientific consensus on climate change. Like all other groups, it is in their interest to preserve and maximize their political and economic interests. And this is exactly what they've done. [...] Climate change deniers work under the veneer of scientific rhetoric by providing an "alternate view." By co-opting scientific rhetoric, they can work under the appearance of scientific legitimacy that fails only under close scrutiny. The problem is that, for those who lean politically or economically conservative, there is no incentive to look at the climate change debate with close scrutiny. Several studies have shown that the greatest indicator of someone's belief on climate change is their political affiliation. […] Coupled with the media's tendency to portray the climate change discussion as "still up for debate" by presenting two sides, or to ensure that they have "balanced coverage," it is not surprising that the fight for the acceptance of man-made climate change has been so difficult. [2]

If you can't agree on the scientific or technical nature of a problem, how on earth do you work together on a solution? This is a question being asked by public officials, scientists, educators, and regular citizens alike. Although some public figures are encouraged by the fact that science-related issues are being discussed more frequently in the political arena, other experts lament the politicization of science, particularly when it comes to big issues like climate change. They argue that science is a realm of objective facts and that political influence not only frustrates scientific progress but also makes it more difficult for the public to understand and deal with these types of issues. University of Wisconsin atmospheric scientist Michael Tobin laments:

Politics is almost impervious to learning. And once a scientific field gets swallowed up by politics, it gets a strange double character. Within its core, it continues to make progress, but at its fringes, the progress is successfully concealed, obfuscated by people who will never get the point of anything. [3]

The question of science's role in public policy is one of the central political dilemmas of our time. And given the enormous scale of the issues at stake, it seems unlikely to fade from relevance any time in the near future. The viewpoints in *At Issue: The Role of Science in Public Policy* will examine contemporary perspectives on the relationship between science and public policy.

Notes

1. "Inventing Conflicts of Interest: A History of Tobacco Industry Tactics," by Allan M. Brandt, American Public Health Association, January 2012.
2. "The Attitudes, Rhetoric, and Politics of Scientific Debate," by Adi Melamed, Brown Political Review, March 11, 2017.
3. "The Main Difference Between Science and Politics", by Michael Tobis, planet3.org, November 29, 2011.

The Role of Science in Public Life

Organisation for Economic Cooperation and Development

Founded in 1960 to stimulate economic progress and world trade, the OECD is an intergovernmental economic organization with 35 member countries. It is a forum of countries that describe themselves as committed to democracy and the market economy, providing a platform to compare policy experiences, seek answers to common problems, identify good practices, and coordinate domestic and international policies among its members.

This viewpoint outlines contemporary issues involving the role of science in public life from an international perspective, with a specific focus on the goal of expanding and improving scientific literacy on a global scale. The authors offer suggestions for how scientific literacy could be improved through education, mass media cooperation, public dialogue, and international cooperation. They argue that the best way to allow the public to understand and weigh in on the ethical considerations of biomedical science and other controversial subjects is through developing a public forum.

The General Picture

In today's world, science and technology (S&T) have taken on ever greater importance in daily life, a trend that will continue as we enter the 21st century. They have brought untold advances in medicine, communication, and transportation, making our

"Science and Technology in the Public Eye," Organisation for Economic Cooperation and Development. Reprinted by permission.

everyday world vastly different from that of earlier generations. While they have brought immense benefits, they have also given rise to questions about how they affect our lives, questions which most of the population, even in advanced countries, lacks the scientific background to address. This leads to a somewhat paradoxical situation: the public generally recognises the value of science and technology but, at the same time, does not adequately understand the issues related to or arising from them.

In particular, there are insufficient, and not always effective, opportunities for leaders, social groups, and the general public to participate together in making strategic S&T choices and to take advantage of scientific expertise in order to understand certain crucial issues with broad-ranging social consequences: the location of nuclear power plants and the disposal of nuclear wastes, blood contaminated with the HIV virus, BSE or "mad cow" disease, the planting or use of transgenic plants as food and, more generally, recombinant DNA field tests, genetic testing, cloning, the uses of information technologies, etc.

With some exceptions, such as research on certain diseases, the general public's support for science and technology is often lukewarm. Yet today, government efforts on behalf of research and development (R&D) are coming under scrutiny or being reduced owing to the serious budgetary restrictions that presently affect almost all industrialised countries. Moreover, in many countries, young people show less interest in studies and careers in the so-called "hard" sciences and in technology than in the past. If this trend continues, it will have serious consequences for maintaining sufficient numbers of researchers in the coming decade as large bodies of researchers retire. Finally, the general population's technical culture appears very inadequate. This is particularly serious among young people, those who will need to work in economies that will be strongly – and increasingly – affected by rapid technical change.

[…]

Looking to the Future

What more needs to be done? What needs to be done better to improve education and motivation, to encourage dialogue and engagement? These are the questions that concern policy makers today. The following areas might usefully be targeted in order to improve scientific literacy and better integrate science and technology into the knowledge-based society:

- Early education: The importance of early education to scientific literacy and to interest in science and technology has been demonstrated. Governments should therefore consider means to ensure better involvement of teachers, improve student motivation, and implement teaching methods based on concrete, "hands-on" learning.
- Life-long learning: Continuing advances in science and technology mean that citizens need to keep abreast of developments and to maintain their interest. More extensive annual science weeks, as well as science museums and science centres with stimulating exhibits elaborated in collaboration with educators and scientists, using the latest possibilities offered by the new media, need to be developed.
- Effective mass media: The effectiveness of the mass media, particularly television, in increasing awareness of science needs to be assessed, with a view to developing attractive, useful materials with genuine scientific content. The potential of the Internet also needs to be harnessed.
- Forums for dialogue: Appropriate institutional arrangements for enhancing public dialogue on science- and technology-related issues, including ethical questions, need to be established or extended.
- International co-operation: All countries can gain from the exchange of high-quality materials (television programmes, exhibits, etc.), as well as from the exchange of types of efforts that have proved successful. It is important to involve scientists and citizens in less developed countries as well, in activities related both to improvement of

primary education in science and to awareness among the adult public, particularly in areas of global interest such as the environment.

There is no doubt that motivation is the primary factor in increasing interest in science and technology. It is obvious that people of all ages learn more easily about any topic, even a very complex one, when they are directly and personally involved. For example, in the face of illness, they quickly learn, and understand, even extremely subtle physiological mechanisms and relevant scientific information. In seeking to help improve scientific literacy, it is therefore necessary to address not only the intelligence but also the imagination and the emotions, in order to make science and technology understandable, as they are only when one has understood that one can make a valid contribution to discussions of science and technology.

Scientists and Engineers

Scientists and engineers should engage actively in public debate about their professional work, both directly and by contributing to the activities of professional interpreters and educators. They should discuss their work and its possible social implications in language that is easy to understand and with a minimum of scientific terminology. They should recognised the validity of informed public attitudes towards specific aspects of their work that may not fully accord with prevailing scientific consensus or industrial preferences.

They should endeavour, through both formal teaching and informal outreach activities, to stimulate young people to explore the frontiers of knowledge, in recognition of the fact that the next generation must continue to advance those frontiers.

They should receive recognition from their peers that public outreach activities involving their work and their discipline are of value, and these efforts should be rewarded in terms of career advancement. As their involvement in such activities is essential, it should be recognised that they may require training in order to participate more effectively in public awareness efforts.

The scientific community should be well informed about the possible ethical and social impact of scientific research and new technologies, sensitive to public concerns and prepared to discuss the ethical issues.

The Public

Instead of simply accepting or rejecting new developments in science and technology, individual citizens have an obligation to gain sufficient knowledge and understanding to express their concerns rationally. They have the right, no less than the responsibility, to express and discuss their concerns, even when they appear to conflict with accepted scientific viewpoints.

Because science and technology contribute to social development and stability, they are the common assets of humankind. Therefore, the public also has a responsibility to nurture skilled human resources able to continue to ensure scientific and technical development.

The Media

Beyond providing appropriate information in response to public uncertainties and concerns associated with science and technology, the media should encourage and facilitate public debate and help scientists and engineers understand the origins and character of public concerns.

The media will increasingly be expected to act as interpreter, conveying specialist knowledge to the public in an easily digested form. While such information will of necessity be cast in accessible, non-scientific language, particular care should be taken to ensure that it is accurate and to point out clearly scientific and technical uncertainties and points of contention if and when they exist.

It is important to disseminate methods of scientific thinking based on critical analysis and continual questioning as well as scientific knowledge. This will improve understanding of research, as well as what can be expected from scientific research, including both its hopes and its limitations.

Governments

Governments should support the building and networking of interactive science centres and museums, the establishment of structural links between these institutions, schools and universities, and support volunteers working in the field of science popularisation. They can also encourage the exchange of high-quality science and technology television and video programmes and the dissemination of scientific and technical information over the Internet. They should also promote international co-operation in line with the ongoing globalisation of information.

Political leaders themselves, as well as technical and administrative managers, need to understand what is at stake in decision making requiring scientific expertise. Decision makers, like the public at large, need to understand not only scientific facts, but also the scientific method (hypothesis, testing, experimentation, validation).

The processes involved in science and technology policy formulation must be transparent. Mission-oriented research involving large groups of scientists or engineers and requiring substantial public funding should be based on public consensus, and suitable techniques for evaluating public research and development activities should be developed.

Governments should also support the building and networking of interactive science centres and museums, the establishment of structural links between these institutions and schools and universities, and support volunteers working in the field of science popularisation. They can also encourage the exchange of high-quality science and technology television and video programmes and the dissemination of scientific and technical information over the Internet. They should also promote international co-operation in line with the ongoing globalisation of information.

Education should provide young people with opportunities to learn the intrinsic value of science and technology and the scientific way of thinking through practical experience and experimentation. It is vital that young people with the potential to become productive scientists recognise the joys of scientific knowledge and creativity. More generally, young people will need to have basic notions of science and technology, in view of their increasing importance for entering the job market and meeting the demand for increasing levels of technical skills. Special attention should be paid to the important role of teachers and curricula, together with parents and local communities, so that students retain the interest in science and technology developed during their formative years. Supporting teachers in developing new approaches to teaching and learning at both the primary and secondary levels is crucial.

As ethical issues become more complex and more evident, particularly in the biomedical sciences, greater efforts to promote public dialogue will be needed to deal with society's legitimate concerns about the science and technology enterprise.

2

The Ethical Considerations of Science Education

Theodore D. Goldfarb and Michael S. Pritchard

Theodore D. Goldfarb is a professor of chemistry at SUNY-Stony Brook. Michael S. Pritchard is a professor of philosophy at Western Michigan University.

This viewpoint offers a contemporary perspective on teaching ethics in science and discusses the history of scientific reasoning in philosophy and other academic disciplines. Since science is the product of human activity, Goldfarb and Pritchard assert that complete objectivity is impossible, and as such ethics should be an important consideration in the field of science. They also argue that it is important to keep motivations and ethical considerations in mind when reviewing scientific research.

[…]

How Ethics and Values Intersect With Science
The Roles of Ethics in Science

A book devoted to advocating the infusion of ethics/values into the teaching of science rests on the assumption that ethics and values play a significant role in science and that ignoring this fact will diminish a student's comprehension of the true nature of the scientific enterprise. But this is not an assumption that is accepted and appreciated by most secondary school students, nor by all of their teachers. When asked about the connection between ethics

"Ethics in the Science Classroom," by Theodore D. Goldfarb and Michael S. Pritchard, National Academy of Sciences. Reprinted by permission.

and science, many science teachers will make reference to such issues as scientific fraud and plagiarism that have occasionally made dramatic headlines. They will generally view such behavior as the exception rather than the rule and profess a belief that science is for the most part an objective and value-free activity practiced by honest, moral individuals. Our point is not to deny that fraudulent behavior among scientists is unusual, but rather to emphasize the fact that science is the product of human activity, and as such it inevitably involves a wide variety of value-laden choices and judgements, many of which have ethical dimensions.

What is science? Professor John Ziman of the Imperial College of Science and Technology, London, one of the most influential writers on the practice of science, points out that definitions given by professional scientists, historians of science, philosophers of science, and representatives of other related disciplines tend to emphasize "different aspects of the subject, often with quite different policy implications." Philosophers might emphasize the methodological aspects of science focusing on experimentation, observation and theorizing as elements of the means by which reliable information about the natural world is gleaned through the practice of science. Historians are prone to view science as the accumulation of knowledge, stressing its archival aspect as a significant historical process worthy of special study. Ziman concludes that: "...science is all these things and more. It is indeed the product of research; it does employ characteristic methods; it is an organized body of knowledge; it is a means of solving problems."

The fact that the practice of science is a human social activity is a central theme of a booklet entitled "On Being a Scientist," initially published in 1989. This booklet was written by the Committee on the Conduct of Science under the auspices of the National Academy of Sciences as a description of the scientific enterprise for students who are about to begin to do scientific research. The reader is instructed that:

> *Scientists have a large body of knowledge that they can use in making decisions. Yet much of this knowledge is not the product*

of scientific investigation, but instead involves value-laden judgements, personal desires, and even a researcher's personality and style.

Debunked is the notion of a rigid Baconian scientific method by which scientists derive truth about the universe by making observations with no preconceptions about what they may discover. Instead the authors claim that:

...research is as varied as the approaches of individual researchers. Some scientists postulate many hypotheses and systematically set about trying to weed out the weaker ones. Others describe their work as asking questions of nature: "What would happen if ...? Why is it that...?" Some researchers gather a great deal of data with only a vague idea about the problem they might be trying to solve. Others develop a specific hypothesis or conjecture that they then try to verify or refute with carefully structured observations. Rather than following a single scientific method, scientists use a body of methods particular to their work.

The booklet includes several real-life stories that illustrate the fallibility of scientists, and the ways in which they can be influenced by personal or social values. Mentioned as examples of the values that can distort science are attitudes regarding religion, race and gender. Assurance is given that science has social structures and mechanisms that tend to limit and correct the influences of such biases. The peer review process, the requirement that experiments be replicable and the openness of communication are claimed to serve this purpose. The booklet ends with a strong appeal for scientists to exercise social responsibility. A second edition of this booklet, revised by a joint committee of the National Academy of Sciences, the National Academy of Engineering and the Institute of Medicine, was published in 1995 and retains much of the discussion of the role of values in science.

The claim that the peer review process and openness of communication significantly reduce the influences of bias in science assumes a set of historic norms for the behavior of scientists that are less descriptive of scientific behavior today than when they were codified by the eminent sociologist R. K. Merton in 1942. Merton's norms, as expressed by Ziman include the principles of communalism (that science is public knowledge available to all), universalism (there are no privileged sources of scientific knowledge), and disinterestedness (science is done for its own sake). In today's world, where the vast majority of scientific research is funded by corporate or other private interests which often place rigid restrictions on the publication of scientific results and the exchange of scientific information, and where academic scientists find themselves in a highly competitive environment, these norms can no longer be viewed as generally applicable to the practice of science.

The tendency of many scientists and teachers of science to portray science and scientists in an idealistic and unrealistic manner is often motivated by belief that this will result in a greater willingness on the part of students and the public to accept scientific, rational thought as a powerful tool for learning about, and understanding, the world and the universe. There is no evidence to support this view. On the contrary, when students are taught that scientists are mere mortals who are subject to the same social pressures and temptations, in their work as well as in their private lives, that influence all human endeavor, they are more likely to identify with scientists. The powerful methods that science offers for seeking knowledge about the universe then become personally accessible rather then a set of exotic tools available only to the members of an elite priesthood.

Recent surveys have shown that despite a renewed interest in mysticism, and growing concern about the contribution of technological development to environmental degradation, public regard for science and technology remains very high. This is particularly true in the United States and other industrialized nations, but also in the developing world. While a high regard for science is certainly a desirable public attitude, it can be associated with an uncritical acceptance of any conclusion or opinion that is presented in the name of science. This is contrary to the essence of the scientific approach to knowledge, which seeks to engender a critical/skeptical attitude and recognizes that all of the results of science are to be viewed as subject to further verification and revision.

By presenting science to students as the product of the work of fallible human agents, rather than as a body of unassailable factual knowledge about the universe, gleaned by means of value-free observation and deduction, we can teach students proper respect for science, while nurturing an appropriate attitude of skepticism. Bringing scientists down from a pedestal is necessary if students are to recognize their own humble efforts in school science laboratories as requiring the same honesty in the reporting of observations and treatment of data that they assume was employed in the deduction of the scientific knowledge contained in their textbooks.

Examples of Ethics and Values Issues in Science

In an essay entitled "The Ethical Dimensions of Scientific Research" the widely published logician and philosopher of science Nicholas Rescher attacks the view that science is value free, and shows how ethical considerations enter into many aspects of the practice of scientific research. Rescher describes ethical problems and issues in science under several headings. We will use Rescher's headings, describing the major ethical issues that he discusses, and adding a few that he doesn't mention:

Choosing Research Goals

Rescher states, "Perhaps the most basic and pervasive way in which ethical problems arise in connection with the prosecution of scientific research is in regard to the choice of research problems, the setting of research goals, and the allocation of resources (both human and material) to the prosecution of research efforts." At the national level, he asks whether we are morally justified in committing such a large fraction of the federal research budget to space exploration at the expense of larger appropriations for the advancement of knowledge in medicine, agriculture and other fields of technology bearing directly on human welfare. Other major value- laden choices that he doesn't mention are the balance between the funding of nuclear energy investigations as opposed to those involving renewable energy sources. A recent issue that has divided the public, politicians and the scientific community is the extent to which "BIG SCIENCE" projects like the supercollider subatomic particle accelerator or the Human Genome Project should be funded as compared to funding a broader variety of more modest "small" science endeavors.

At the institutional level of the department, laboratory or research institute, Rescher mentions the issue of support for pure, or basic, versus applied, or practical, research. Today, with an increasing fraction of research being done by, or funded by, industry the constraints imposed by corporate interests on the choice of research projects, or on the direction of the research is becoming an increasingly significant ethical issue.

At the individual level Rescher cites difficult, and even painful, ethical decisions that often must be made. These include the choice between pure and, frequently more lucrative, applied research, and for those who choose applied science, such questions as whether to work on military projects. Recently the media have publicized the moral dilemma of whether former researchers for the tobacco industry should violate secrecy agreements by revealing that the industry knew more about the addictive nature of nicotine than was claimed in sworn testimony by company spokespeople.

Staffing of Research Activities
Rescher includes under this heading the ethical concerns that arise when scientists become administrators of large sums of public money that are needed to fund most forms of contemporary scientific research. As he points out, the increasing administrative responsibilities imposed on scientists is an ethical issue, in and of itself, because it impairs a scientist's ability to devote his or her energies to the practice of science. In research at universities, the employment of graduate students to do research raises issues about whether the assigned research is the optimal work in terms

of the education and the training of the student. An additional ethical concern related to staffing a research group is the fact that women and minority members have historically been under-represented in scientific research. Making good on commitments to equal opportunity is a serious moral obligation of the scientist as research administrator.

Research Methods

The ethical concerns related to the use of human subjects and animals in research are the focus of Rescher's remarks about issues related to the methods of research. The heightened public concern about animals as research subjects resulting from the animal rights movement is an issue familiar to most science teachers, particularly biology teachers. The deletion of experiments using animals in school science laboratories, due to moral objections by teachers, students, parents or the community, is becoming an increasingly common occurrence.

Other ethics and values issues related to research methods include such questions as whether a double-blind protocol is needed in cases where subjective interpretations of research data may influence experimental results. Additionally, there are issues related to the manipulation and presentation of data. The use of placebos in tests of the effectiveness of a new drug can raise ethical issues associated with the withholding of a potentially effective treatment of a serious illness.

Standards of Proof and Dissemination of Research Findings

Rescher discusses the issue of the amount of evidence a scientist must accumulate before announcing his or her findings. As he states, "This problem of standards of proof is ethical, and not merely theoretical or methodological in nature, because it bridges the gap between scientific understanding and action, between thinking and doing..." Personal factors, such as the need to publish in order to advance his or her career goals may tempt a scientist to exaggerate the certainty of scientific results. The fact that positive results are often rewarded by increased funding from research sponsors increases this temptation.

In most cases, the science establishment scorns the scientist who chooses to announce his or her findings via public media before they have been published in a peer- reviewed journal. As discussed by Rescher, there is good reason to be concerned about premature publicity about findings that have not been accepted as valid by the scientific community. Well known researchers or research institutions can use the sensationalism, which is as much a characteristic of science reporting as other types of journalism, to influence public opinion and governmental funding agencies. The media emphasis on such values as the novel and the spectacular which, if translated into more funds for this type of study, can distort the development of science.

Other types of ethical conflict, not mentioned by Rescher, may result from publication standards. A scientist may be convinced that the results of a study are valid, and may have significant, perhaps even urgent, social value, although they do not quite meet the often rigid standards set by his or her peers. One such standard is the generally accepted requirement that in order to be considered valid, a result derived from statistical analysis of data must have less than a 5% chance of being a result of chance. Suppose a scientist analyzes some geological data that show that some natural disaster is likely to occur at the 93% rather than the 95% statistical confidence level. No possibility exists of doing further studies that might increase the certainty of the result. Peer reviewers at the relevant scientific journal reject the report because it fails the 95% test. The scientist must make the decision whether to accept this judgment or risk the opprobrium of colleagues and make the results known by seeking the help of news-hungry science journalists.

Control of Scientific "Misinformation"

Rescher affirms that scientists have a duty to control and suppress scientific misinformation. This obligation extends to preventing erroneous research findings from misleading their colleagues and, perhaps more urgently, to protect against the danger that false results may endanger the health or welfare of the public.

On the other hand, Rescher warns against misusing this need to censor misinformation in a way that stifles novelty and innovation. Too often in the history of science, scientists, particularly those who are young and not yet well-established, have found it very difficult to gain acceptance for revolutionary discoveries that do not fit within the prevailing disciplinary paradigm.

Rescher also raises the issue of science versus pseudo-science. Whereas the need to control misinformation would logically extend to pseudo-science, he points out that the distinction between what is accepted as science and what some members of the scientific community would label as pseudo-science is not always clear. As examples of contemporary problems in this area are the scientific standing of various forms of extra-sensory perception, herbal and other non-Western, "traditional" medicines, acupuncture and the recent controversy over the validity of "cold fusion." Rescher urges caution to those who would settle such disputes through censorship and suppression of views that they fear might damage the public image of science. He suggests, instead that scientists have faith that truth will "...win out in the market place of freely interchanged ideas..."

[…]

3

Scientific Standards Should Be Set in the Courtroom

Sanne H. Knudsen

Sanne H. Knudsen is an assistant professor of law at the University of Washington School of Law.

In this viewpoint, Knudsen argues in favor of scientific standards developed through litigation. She explains the unique aspects of science-driven public policy through the example of natural resource damage assessment (NRDA) projects. In these cases, politics, law, and science come together to evaluate the impacts of an environmental disaster, demonstrating the ways in which science and law can coexist and complement one another.

While no one hopes for environmental disasters, a great deal can be learned from them. In fact, much of what we know of long-term ecological exposure to toxins comes from studies undertaken in the wake of massive oil spills like the *Exxon Valdez* or the *Deepwater Horizon*. In many ways, these events—though unfortunate—present an unparalleled opportunity to intensely study the effects of toxic exposure to ecosystems. Laboratories, for instance, cannot replicate the conditions often needed to study the complex response of ecosystems to toxins. Though inordinately complicated, the ecological conditions created post-*Exxon Valdez* or post-*Deepwater Horizon* allow for real-time observation of the

"Adversarial Science," by Sanne H. Knudsen, Iowa Law Review, 2015. Reprinted by permission.

intricate and entangled ways that ecosystems are impacted by toxic exposure. The political support for intensive scientific inquiry is also piqued in the wake of mass-disaster events. Media attention and public outcry combine to create a demand for comprehensive study that may otherwise have less enthusiastic political support.

As an example of the informational opportunities created by mass-disaster events, consider the intense study of the Gulf of Mexico that is currently underway to determine the nature and magnitude of injuries caused by the 2010 *Deepwater Horizon* oil spill. Technical working groups consisting of government, academic, and industry scientists have been assembled to study the ecological impacts of oil spills on a wide variety of species and their habitats, from mudflats to corral. For each affected resource and habitat, the scientific inquiry is cumbersome and detailed. Some scientists are tasked with evaluating the impacts of oil and chemical dispersants on representative groups of aquatic species. To do so, they must consider a range of exposure pathways, including "oil droplets . . . oiled sediment, and ingestion of contaminated prey [or] food." Other studies are focused on enhancing knowledge of deepwater communities, which first requires "[m]apping soft- and hard-bottom habitats along the continental shelf and sea floor." The amount of scientific data being generated from this collective research is massive, so much that specialized support teams have been assembled to create and manage information databases.

Importantly, the study in the wake of these disasters is not just short-lived. There is increasingly a focus on studying the long-term, chronic impacts. After the *Deepwater Horizon* spill, government trustees have declared their commitment "to a long-term assessment of the Gulf, recognizing that the *Deepwater Horizon* oil spill will affect the region's natural resources for years to come." This is an area where deep study is historically lacking.

While certainly intensive, there may be an important caveat to the learning opportunities presented by events like the *Exxon Valdez* or *Deepwater Horizon* spills. Notably, these extensive scientific studies are undertaken through a process known as natural resource damage assessment ("NRDA"). Government trustees prepare NRDAs in the wake of oil spills and toxic-substance releases. Trustees use these assessments to identify the nature and extent of injuries resulting from the release so that the government can make claims for natural resource damages against the responsible party. Ultimately, natural resource damage awards are used to fund restoration projects that will return injured public resources to baseline conditions.

At its core, then, NRDA is an adversarial process. To be sure, because natural resource damages awards are used to restore injured public resources, the science developed to support NRDA claims may not reflexively conjure concerns of litigation science, at least not in any mass tort sense. Nonetheless, both government trustees and corporate defendants, like BP and Exxon, are driven by political and economic, as well as scientific, agendas. Because of that, scientific studies undertaken during the NRDA process raise questions of conflicts of interest and bias that are inherent in litigation-generated science. Indeed, while legal scholars have not examined NRDA science as a form of adversarial science, some scientists have outright questioned the advocacy embedded in NRDA studies.

So what can be done when one of the most important sources of science on the complexity of ecological harms—at least in terms of volume and opportunity—is also born from litigation? The short answer is: use it. More specifically, NRDA science should be embraced as an immensely useful source of understanding ecological harms from both acute and chronic toxic exposure. But, only after its risks are understood and institutional controls have been developed to ensure its legitimacy.

Often the science-litigation interface evokes thoughts of *Daubert*, "junk science," and discussions about the competency of courts to fulfill their gatekeeping role.

Indeed, the term "litigation science" made its jurisprudential debut in Judge Kozinski's *Daubert* opinion. Scholars and courts have since grappled with litigation science and its treatment under

Daubert; some have cast doubt on its veracity as compared to other bodies of science. By contrast, this Article critiques the discourse that diminishes scientific knowledge merely because it emerges in a litigation, or adversarial, context. The real story is much more complicated.

This Article starts with the idea that litigation science plays an important informational role in understanding long-term ecological injuries. In that sense, the questions raised here go beyond *Daubert*; they go beyond the issue of judging litigation science in the courtroom. The aim is not gatekeeping experts or sorting junk science from real science in any one case. Rather, the goal is to optimize the use of adversarial science in informing broader public health and environmental policy choices well after litigation files have been closed.

To further the goal of filling the science gap with good science, Part II examines why adversarial science has an important role to play in understanding ecological injuries. Part II also surveys the literature and considers whether adversarial science is different from other forms of policy-relevant science.

After exploring why adversarial science should be permitted or even encouraged to fill the knowledge gap on toxic exposure, Part III takes a critical look at NRDA science as a product of advocacy. It uses the scientific literature in the wake of the *Exxon* spill to identify three fundamental ways in which litigation influences NRDA science. Part IV builds on these categories of influence by examining the particular structural challenges that arise when assessing long-term harms.

Ultimately, this Article is as much about promise as risk. To that end, Part V proposes solutions that optimize the ability of NRDA science to advance scientific understanding of long-term ecological injuries in the wake of chronic toxic exposure. It examines some ways in which regulatory controls can be used to harness NRDA science and legitimize it for use beyond the courtroom. In particular, these solutions encourage the development of long-term scientific study while ensuring that the science is reliable enough to shape policy and inform understanding outside the particular litigation context in which it was developed.

By using NRDA science to describe both the benefits and challenges of adversarial science, this Article shifts the discussion from one of mere castigation and skepticism to one of optimism. In particular, it opens the door to future discussions about how courtroom and litigation controls might be harnessed to enhance the legitimacy of adversarial science outside the courtroom.

The Promise of Adversarial Science

Why is it desirable to encourage reliance on science that is developed in a litigation context? After all, one natural response to adversarial science might simply be to write it off as adversarial posturing. However, there are at least two problems with casting adversarial science aside. First, adversarial science may be necessary to advance understanding of ecological harms in under-studied areas like toxic exposure.

Second, adversarial science might not be inherently biased (or at least not any more so than other forms of policy-oriented science), but instead, it might simply be perceived as such. If true, these would both be reasons to embrace adversarial science from NRDA proceedings.

The Necessity of Litigation Science

When it comes to the effects of toxic exposure, there is a significant science gap on issues of whether toxins cause harm and, if so, in what form. These science gaps have led some scholars to observe that there is a fundamental failure of regulatory regimes to encourage the systematic study of toxic exposure.

The study of long-term toxic exposure presents even more challenges. Popular media and science literature readily recognize that questions of long-term injuries are inherently complicated because of chronic exposure to toxins in everyday life.

In some areas of research, like studies examining impacts to marine ecosystems following oil spills, the scientific literature is starting to recognize that long-term harms can be even more significant than short-term acute injuries. But, as with long-term injuries to humans from toxic exposure, time lags, synergistic effects, and complicated biological interdependencies make it difficult to understand long-term injury to ecosystems. Tracing causal pathways and differentiating between multiple contributing stressors is a particularly difficult problem. In the toxic torts area, these challenges have given rise to a rich body of legal literature discussing the problems of proof and examining alternate causal frameworks for latent injuries.

As long as the regulatory process creates or tolerates gaps in knowledge, logic dictates that adversarial science will be developed to offer proof of harm. The gap in scientific knowledge on issues of toxic exposure, and the potential of NRDA science to fill those gaps for ecological injuries, makes an active embrace of litigation science worth considering. One area well-known for its science gap is long-term injury and toxic torts, where causal relationships between toxic exposure and human or ecological injury are poorly understood. What are the consequences of chronic and sustained exposure to benzene in the workplace? How might chronic use of anti-bacterial soap by children cause endocrine or hormonal problems later in life? What are the long-term impacts of oil spills on the marine ecosystem? How are pesticides in groundwater impacting human endocrine systems? These are questions that could benefit most from sustained research, but may never undergo systematic study as part of any coordinated regulatory regime.

The ad hoc nature of research on harms from chronic chemical or toxic exposure is at least partially responsible for the gaps in scientific knowledge. In her work, Professor Wendy Wagner examines the "dearth of research and basic information" available on how industrial activities affect health and the environment. In doing so, she explains that "[v]irtually every prominent expert panel convened to consider the effects" have expressed alarm as to the lack of information. This regulatory gap is one reason why litigation science exists and plays a key role in the development of scientific understanding of long-term toxic exposure. In fact, litigation and the potential for damage awards provide the financial incentive to undertake studies to fill in those gaps.

Wagner's work further suggests that the regulatory gap is not likely to go away simply because it has been identified. To that end, in suggesting some theories as to why the regulatory gap exists, Wagner explains that "when the stakes are high, actors not only will resist producing potentially incriminating information but [also] will invest in discrediting public research that suggests their activities are harmful." Wagner's observation suggests that litigation might force the hand of chemical or other product manufacturers who might otherwise prefer control over access to potentially damaging information. Litigation and its tools of discovery can serve truth-seeking and information-forcing functions that current regulatory regimes may lack. In fact, Professor Sheila Jasanoff has recognized the promise of litigation science for testing knowledge: "[B]ecause litigation itself is such a powerful prod to producing new scientific evidence, adversarial legal processes sometimes provide the only significant testing ground for claims relevant to settling disputes."

NRDA science might be especially valuable for reducing the regulatory and science gaps. NRDA science has made substantial contributions to understanding ecological injuries. In the wake of the *Exxon Valdez* oil spill, for instance, scientific studies regarding the lingering effects of the oil reveal that the long-term consequences of toxic exposure might be even more substantial than the acute, graphic injuries. Similarly, the *Deepwater Horizon* spill presents unique opportunities for studying the ecosystem response to both acute and chronic toxic exposure. Consider, for example, that researchers have suddenly found themselves in the middle of an intensive, coordinated, interdisciplinary and highly visible effort to study deepwater communities in the wake of the *Deepwater Horizon* spill. This is a resource for which there has historically been "limited knowledge." Now researchers are doing everything from mapping the location of habitats on the sea floor, to assessing the potential toxicity for deepwater habitats exposed to oil, to studying impacts on community composition and reproductive responses. For other resources as well, researchers are busy examining the toxicological responses of aquatic species in a wide range of habitats, from wetlands to coral.

Some NRDA science, like mapping or other resource inventories, can be undertaken in the absence of an oil spill. After the *Deepwater Horizon* spill, for instance, researchers are surveying the sea floor to "confirm the presence of deepwater coral communities." For this work, the oil spill creates a discrete need, but the research could be done any time there is sufficient desire and funding. Notably, however, the desire to fund this type of inventorying or purely descriptive science may not exist absent an acute need for information, as evidenced by the *Deepwater Horizon* spill itself.

Other NRDA science, however, arises from the unique opportunity to examine impacts to an entire ecosystem as they unfold in the short and long term. After an oil spill, the entire affected ecosystem becomes a laboratory. In this way, NRDA science provides a rare chance to study first-hand the resilience of marine ecosystems and to sort out the synergistic implications of multiple stressors that otherwise combine to affect change. Moreover, the NRDA scientific programs are extensive and have the potential for systematic, coordinated, and multi-disciplinary studies of a single marine ecosystem.

Sometimes, the studies are undertaken over many decades and provide significant insight into the nature of long-term harms. In these ways, NRDA science will necessarily make a substantial contribution to the collective scientific understanding of toxic exposure and marine ecosystems. Indeed, the catastrophic nature of oil spills, public outcry, and inherently reactive nature of NRDA combine to create opportunities for scientific study that cannot be fully replicated outside of the crisis setting. The natural resource damage context is therefore one area where litigation science plays an information role that cannot simply be filled by regulatory regimes.

In the end, the value added from the NRDA process amounts to more than just arriving at a dollar figure for damages. In fact, it is destructive to think that the vast amount of science NRDA generates can be discarded simply because it emerges from an adversarial context. Doing so would undermine the broader public interest in understanding ecological effects from acute and chronic toxic exposure. A better approach is to assess how NRDA science is influenced by its adversarial context and propose solutions to legitimize the science or the perception of the science. This approach serves the dual goals of advancing the state of knowledge and ensuring the integrity of that knowledge.

Comparing Adversarial Science to Other Policy-Relevant Science

Just because adversarial science fills an information gap does not alone mean it should be embraced. Indeed, for information to be useful, it must also be reliable. To that end, we ought to pause for a moment to consider whether science born out of litigation is inherently more suspect than other forms of policy-relevant science. If we find the veracity of adversarial science particularly suspect, we might prefer to explore other mechanisms for generating the necessary information.

Importantly, many scholars have deeply considered the complicated intersections of policy and science. In doing so, they have grappled with the legitimacy concerns that arise when science is used to advance a particular public policy or regulatory agenda, albeit outside the litigation context. They have questioned whether science can in fact be separated from the policy judgments that are inextricably intertwined with risk management decisions. They have examined uncertainty inherent in science, paying special attention to efforts by some stakeholders to use or manufacture uncertainty as a means of avoiding regulation.

Even when popular audiences, scientists, and politicians have called for the revival of "sound science" in regulatory decision-making, scholars have questioned whether any science that is used in setting public policy can really be deemed "pure science." Indeed, well-known scholars like Professor Sheila Jasanoff have long argued that even the act of labeling science as "pure science" or "policy-relevant science" is a contested exercise shaped by institutional and political interests.

In the area of natural resources law, Professor Holly Doremus has described the related phenomena where agencies make policy decisions in the name of science in order to avoid scrutiny. She explains that "[t]he core of the problem is not the involvement of politics but its concealment behind a cloak of science." Professor Wendy Wagner has made similar observations in the toxic regulation context, unveiling a "science charade" where "agencies exaggerate the contributions made by science in setting toxic standards in order to avoid accountability for the underlying policy decisions." These observations are consistent with Jasanoff's assertion that labels matter in terms of public perception; for Doremus and Wagner, the desire to label policy decisions as scientific ones motivates agencies to shape their rationales around science. This phenomenon has lead Doremus to call for greater transparency in regulatory decisions in order to make clear when science stops and policy starts.

Many solutions have been proposed, including increasing transparency in regulatory decisions, allowing access to federally funded research data, instituting greater regulatory peer review, reexamining the reliance on scientific advisory committees, and imposing *Daubert*-like review on agency decisions.

In some ways, the challenges of litigation science are similar to science generated in the regulatory context. In neither context is the science "pure." The science is undertaken with a particular purpose in mind, whether that purpose is setting policy at a regulatory level or providing evidence of injury. There may also be a propensity to generate uncertainty as a way of manipulating the outcome. In the regulatory sphere, scientific uncertainty is one tool for combatting additional regulatory oversight. In the litigation context, defendants have a particular incentive to generate uncertainty as a way of undermining the plaintiffs' ability to meet their burden of proof on issues like causation. And finally, in both contexts, funding imbalances may affect the ability of certain stakeholders to generate more or high levels of science to advance their positions. Regardless of whether empirical data would bear out those claims, there may at least be a perception that corporations have greater funding available to generate science to advance their desired outcomes. Those perceptions may matter.

For all these reasons, science produced in the anticipation of litigation does not raise entirely unique concerns. Many influential scholars have observed the competing influences and agendas that shape policy-relevant science. Some of those observations apply to adversarial science as well. And yet, science produced in the adversarial context ought at least be examined on its own terms. To be sure, despite the general similarities between adversarial science and other forms of policy-relevant science, there are also differences. These differences are largely driven by the culture of litigation as an acceptable forum to battle with a narrow purpose— winning for individual gain. Plaintiffs who are able to prove injury through the help of science stand to gain greater monetary awards. Defendants, too, have immediate financial incentives. Litigation is typically a private enterprise, with clear winners and losers, and set in a reactive frame where, ultimately, liability will be judged and damages awarded. By the very nature of its focused and reactive frame, litigation is less searching and less concerned with community outcomes. The parties are expected to advance their best positions and attempt to rebut contradictory evidence. The parties are not expected to objectively examine the evidence and present a measured view of their case.

By contrast, regulatory science is generated to advance a public policy or public health objective. Notwithstanding differing opinions on what public policy decision might be preferable, and notwithstanding the self-interest that nonetheless drives some decisions (e.g., getting a new drug approved by the FDA), the regulatory conversation is framed from the perspective of advancing a public purpose.

In the end, these differences may do more to shape perception than anything else. In fact, there are reasons to think that adversarial science, though different in some respects, might not be vastly more prone to manipulation than other forms of policy-relevant science. After all, adversarial science is subject to controls that are not part of the regulatory process. For example, experts advancing adversarial science are subject to cross-examination and evidentiary rules. Science developed outside the litigation context provides no guarantee of purity or lack of bias. If that is true, adversarial science may not be worth dismissing out of hand. In other words, if litigation science is not uniquely plagued by self-interest, it cannot fairly be dismissed on that basis unless all policy-oriented science undergoes similar castigation.

[...]

4

Effective Communication with the Public Is Necessary for Scientific Awareness

Frank J. Kelly and Julia C. Fussell

Frank J. Kelly and Julia C. Fussell are scientists affiliated with the NIHR Health Protection Unit in Health Impact of Environmental Disasters of the MRC-PHE Centre for Environment and Health at Kings College in London.

Using air pollution as a case study, the viewpoint authors explore how scientific awareness depends on the effectiveness of public communication channels, which are an outgrowth of politics and government dynamics. When there is a symbiotic relationship between these communities, regulatory action can have a positive impact on public health and health awareness. They assert that proper monitoring and reporting of air pollution are necessary for public awareness, and that requiring that this information be made available to the public helps increase the chances of a public health concern being addressed.

Historical Perspective

Air pollution is now fully acknowledged to be a significant public health problem, responsible for a growing range of health effects that are well documented from the results of an extensive research effort conducted in many regions of the world. Whilst there is no doubt that rapid urbanisation means that we are now exposed to unhealthy concentrations and a more diverse variety of ambient

"Air pollution and public health: emerging hazards and improved understanding of risk," by Frank J. Kelly and Julia C. Fussell, Springer Netherlands, June 4, 2015. https://doi.org/10.1007/s10653-015-9720-1. Licensed under CC BY 4.0 International.

air pollutants, palaeopathological research suggests the problem, in the form of smoke, plagued our oldest ancestors. Computerised tomography imaging studies on the bodies of ancient mummies have detected evidence of pneumonia, emphysema, pulmonary oedema and atherosclerosis (Zweifel et al. 2009; Thompson et al. 2013), whilst autopsies have described extensive carbon deposits in the lung (Zimmerman et al. 1971). This in turn has led to a speculative link to the daily inhalation of smoke in confined spaces from fuels used for warmth, cooking and lighting.

Leaping forward through history to Victorian London, the billowing smoke and sulphur dioxide (SO_2) from domestic and industrial coal burning, mixed with natural fog, famously caught the imagination of literary and visual artists. They regarded this meteorological phenomenon as a spectacular manifestation of turn-of-the-century life in a cosmopolitan city. Indeed, the unique style that Charles Dickens adopted in his description of the fogs meant that they became a romantic legend. For Claude Monet, the chromatic atmospheric effects created by the effects of smog on sunlight gave London magnificent breadth and became the predominant theme in his renditions of the city. As a consequence, to some, London's notoriously toxic air became a world-famous institution rather than an appalling social evil. In December 1952, however, a vast and lethal smog, caused by cold stagnant weather conditions that trapped combustion products at ground level, brought about the worst air pollution disaster in history, resulting in an estimated 4000–12,000 deaths and an enormous increase in respiratory and cardiovascular complications (Logan 1953; Bell and Davis 2001). This crisis was also the direct incentive to pass the Clean Air Act in 1956, which successfully curtailed domestic coal burning in London and other major cities in the UK. At this point, the UK led the world in cleaning up air by implementing smokeless zones, imposing controls on industry, increasing the availability and use of natural gas and changing the industrial and economic structure of the country. The results were considerable reductions in the concentration of smoke and SO_2 (Wilkins 1954).

Modern-Day Air Pollution

On recounting such progress, it is especially disappointing that in recent years, improvements in air quality, not solely within the UK but in many urban areas around the world, have miserably stalled. We occasionally experience smog hanging over our cities when poor air-flow and dispersal allows pollution to build up—and it is during such episodes that susceptible individuals (e.g. those with asthma, COPD or heart disease) may undergo an acute exacerbation requiring increased medication or admission to hospital. Of greater concern, however, is the inherent, modern type of pollution in today's urban environments, which unlike the Victorian pea-souper smog, is indiscernible at ground level but manifests in chronic health effects. This 'invisible killer' contains nitrogen oxides, ozone (O_3) and exceptionally small particulate matter (PM). PM_{10} and the more abundant $PM_{2.5}$ constitute particles with diameters less than 10 and 2.5 µm, respectively—the latter being approximately 30 times less than the width of human hair. Of the modern-day air pollutants, PM has been held responsible for the majority of health effects. In urban areas, the major source is fossil fuel combustion, primarily from road transport, as well as power stations and factories. In rural and semi-urban areas of developing countries, the burning of biomass fuels on open fires or traditional stoves creates indoor concentrations of PM that far exceed those considered safe in outdoor air.

Over the last 10 years, there has been a substantial increase in findings from many research disciplines (e.g. population exposure, observational epidemiology, controlled exposure studies, animal toxicology and in vitro mechanistic work) that these modern-day ambient pollutants are not only exerting a greater impact on established health endpoints, but are also associated with a broader number of disease outcomes. The aim of this brief review article is to summarise the increased health hazards to emerge from PM air pollution research in recent years, drawing upon findings published in international projects (WHO 2012, 2013a), Health Effects Institute (HEI) research reports (HEI 2010,

2013a, b), authoritative reviews (Brook et al. 2010) and important individual publications. We will also discuss how the increased evidence base of risk relates to current public awareness and understanding of the problem. Indeed, focused education and continued evolution of sophisticated information systems have the potential to achieve a durable change in public attitude and behaviour, in a way that improves people's health as well as the quality of the air they breathe.

[...]

Public Awareness and Education

That poor air quality can have such a significant impact on human health is undisputed, and the previous sections have drawn upon research conducted over recent years that supports the notion that risks are increasing as new hazards emerge. How then does this translate to public awareness of the problem? The general consensus is that society would benefit from being better engaged and educated about the complex relationship between air quality and ill health (Kelly et al. 2012). If people are aware of variations in the quality of the air they breathe, the effect of pollutants on health as well as concentrations likely to cause adverse effects and actions to curtail pollution, there follows a greater likelihood of motivating changes in both individual behaviour and public policy. In turn, such awareness has the potential to create a cleaner environment and a healthier population.

Studies and initiatives examining public awareness and understanding in this area have yielded mixed results, with some acknowledging a significant amount of concern within the public over poor air quality, an awareness of air quality warnings, and a positive relationship between alerts and a change in outdoor activities (DEFRA 2002; Wen et al. 2009; McDermott et al. 2006). In fact, following findings that air quality warnings associated with ground level O_3 do have a significant impact on attendance at outdoor facilities in Southern California, Neidell and Kinney (2010) suggested that ambient air quality measurements from monitors may not reflect personal exposure if individuals intentionally limit their exposure in response poor air quality. Bell et al. (2004) have also hypothesised that deliberate avoidance in time spent outdoors could contribute to the considerable heterogeneity in O_3-induced mortality observed across US communities. Other research has concluded that both awareness of the links between air pollution and ill health and an understanding of air quality information are lacking amongst the public (Bickerstaff and Walker 2001; Semenza et al. 2008; COMEAP 2011). In 2013, the European Commission (EC) conducted a flash Eurobarometer to gain a greater insight into the views of the European public on matters of air quality and air pollution (EC 2013). Six out of ten Europeans responded that they did not feel informed about air quality issues in their country. When asked how serious they considered a range of air quality related problems to be in their country, responses for respiratory disorders, cardiovascular diseases and asthma/allergy were 87, 92 and 87 % respectively.

Factors Determining Awareness

Other than the availability of sufficient information that will be covered in the following section, factors governing how aware individuals are about the quality of their air and potential repercussions for their health are likely to include understanding, perception and a vested interest. Individuals may choose not to concern themselves about air quality owing to a poor understanding of what is undoubtedly a complex science. Unlike other environmental risks that are routinely communicated such as UV and heat, overall air quality encompasses several primary pollutants as well as secondary products owing to atmospheric transformation. Rural areas for example are very often considered safe places to escape from pollution. However, at times, O_3 concentrations can be as high or greater than urban locations owing to the presence of lower concentrations of nitrogen oxides to sequester rural O_3. A lack of vested interest in the topic is also possible amongst 'healthy' people, less likely to have any personal experience of the benefits that lessoning pollution and/or increasing medication may bring. Indeed, where research has indicated that individuals are aware of air quality warnings and take responsive actions, larger responses were observed for more susceptible groups or carers thereof (McDermott et al. 2006; Wen et al. 2009). Within a cross-sectional study of 33,888 adults participating in the 2005 Behavioral Risk Factor Surveillance System, 31 % with asthma versus 16 % without changed outdoor activity in response to media alerts (Wen et al. 2009). Perception is another factor influencing the public understanding of the importance of healthy air, as attitudes and behaviour can be driven by a person's immediate locality and own understanding rather than accurate data generated by monitoring sites and communicated via an advisory service (Shooter and Brimblecombe 2009). Several studies have investigated the relationship between perceived and measured outdoor air quality provided by monitoring stations and whilst some studies found a significant association between the perception of air quality and specific air pollutants (Atari et al. 2009), others have found little or no association (Rotko et al. 2002). Of relevance, Semenza et al. (2008) not only reported a low (10–15 %) level of behavioural change during an air pollution episode, but that the personal perception of poor air quality rather than the advisory service, drove the response. Some epidemiological researchers have also indicated that self-reported health status is associated with perceived air pollution rather than measured air pollution (Lercher et al. 1995; Yen et al. 2006; Piro et al. 2008).

Information Services

Public awareness is fundamentally dependent upon optimal air pollution monitoring, forecasting and reporting. Many countries have air quality monitoring networks that are structured around a particular country's regulatory obligation to report monitored air quality data and modelled predictions (Kelly et al. 2012). Output from measured concentrations of pollutants, air quality modelling systems and meteorological data are also processed to create a national air quality index (AQI). Again in line with national legislation, an AQI communicates pollution levels and health effects likely to be experienced on the day described by the index or days soon afterwards (i.e. the short term). These data are used by the public and organisations (health services and governments) to reduce the health impacts of predicted air pollution. For example, people susceptible to high levels of pollution may be prompted to take actions (reduce exposure and/or increase use of inhaled reliever medication) to reduce their symptoms, and the general public may be encouraged to use public rather than private transport during periods of poor air quality. Another information tool is provided by accessible air pollution alert services that provide real-time data and proactively alert registered users of impending pollution events via a computer/tablet (websites, email, social media) or phone (texts, apps) (London Air Quality Network; City of London). These are becoming increasingly informative and engaging, allowing people to sign up to specific user groups (e.g. cyclist, jogger, business, at risk) and receive notifications when pollution exceeds concentrations at a site(s) of their choice. These services also offer tailored advice on how specific groups can reduce emissions by for example, providing low pollution journey planners to reduce exposure.

New Developments

Whilst monitoring, forecasting and reporting of air quality have become increasingly sophisticated and accurate, the future use of more individualised exposure measurements holds a great deal more potential. Air pollution levels can vary dramatically over short distances and time scales and in addition people's daily mobility and activities will result in variability in exposure and inhalation. As such, AQIs and alert systems sourced by fixed site monitoring stations are always going to be limited by location, spacing and density. Up until recently, the use of personal pollution monitors was primarily limited to industries associated with high occupational exposures and researchers assessing individual exposures in vulnerable groups such as cyclists (Nwokoro et al. 2012) and asthmatic children (Spira-Cohen et al. 2011). Now we are witnessing an emerging role for inexpensive, portable, easy-to-use personal monitoring devices (Austen 2015). Although the quality of information generated by such sensors is not currently robust enough to compliment data for official monitoring networks, there is undoubtedly a need for more dynamic measures of time-activity patterns in relation to exposures. In an initiative to better understand in real time the impacts of harmful air pollutants, the US Environmental Protection Agency awarded a $100,000 prize to designers of a low-cost wearable breathing analysis tool that calculates the amount of polluted air a person breathes and transmits the data to any Bluetooth-enabled device such as a mobile phone (EPA 2013). Smart phone technology, integrated with low-cost air quality sensors, also has the potential to produce dynamic, temporally and spatially more precise exposure measures for the mass population. Added to their ubiquitous technology, the penetration of these phones is unrivalled in demographics, geographic coverage, acceptance and presence in everyday life (Pratt et al. 2012). This opens up new possibilities in the communication of individual exposure and activity data, tailored to locations where people commute and reside. In the environmental research setting, novel smartphone-based software that records people's movements and physical activity levels in the urban environment and is integrated with spatial–temporal maps of air pollution is already being developed to enhance large-scale air pollution exposure data collection in a cost-effective, accurate unobtrusive way (de Nazelle et al. 2013).

Discussion

Despite past improvements in air quality, very large parts of the population in urban areas breathe air that does not meet European standards let alone WHO Air Quality Guidelines. It should not be surprising therefore that health effects of PM—one of the pollutants deemed most dangerous to health—are well documented. Airborne

PM has been the focus of extensive research and debate around the world for several decades and as a consequence, the evidence base for the association between short- and long-term exposure to PM and cardiopulmonary mortality and morbidity has become much larger and broader. DEPs are now classified as carcinogenic, and an increasing number of studies are investigating the potential for particulate air pollution to negatively influence birth outcomes, diabetes, neurodevelopment and cognitive function. We now also appreciate that there is no evidence of a safe level of exposure or a threshold below which no adverse health effects occur, with recent long-term studies are showing associations between PM and mortality at levels well below the current annual WHO air quality guideline level for $PM_{2.5}$. Correspondingly, reductions in population exposure to air pollution expressed as annual average $PM_{2.5}$ or PM_{10} have appreciable benefits in terms of increased life expectancy and improvements to respiratory health.

Having firmly established associations between ambient PM and adverse health effects, there has been an enormous effort to identify what it is in ambient PM that affects health—information that in turn will inform policy makers how best to legislate for cleaner air. The topic of relative toxicity has been the subject of several critical reviews over recent years but despite this the general conclusion remains that the current database of experimental and epidemiologic studies precludes individual characteristics or sources to be definitely identified as critical for toxicity. A better understanding of exposure and health effects plus further progress in comparing and synthesising data from existing studies is therefore needed before concluding that additional indicators (be they BC or UFPs) have a role in protecting public health more effectively than the targeting total PM mass. Another challenge has been to unravel the underlying biological basis of toxicity by identifying pathways that ultimately link pollution-induced pulmonary and systemic oxidative stress with an associated risk of cardiovascular and obstructive pulmonary diseases.

Evidence has emerged that (a) the burden of ambient PM pollution on health is significant at relatively low concentrations, (b) there is no safe lower limit and (c) effects follow a mostly linear concentration–response function, suggesting that public health benefits will result from any reduction in concentrations. As has been advocated many times before, interventions to reduce levels of particulate pollution require a concerted action by a host of sectors with a vested interest in air quality management (environment, transport, energy, health, housing) at regional, national and international levels. The significant toll of ill health brought about by traffic-related particulates means that forward-looking and integrated transport policies are critical for the improvement of urban environments. Traffic must be reduced and we must ensure a cleaner and greener element to what remains on the road. This can be achieved through an expansion of low emission zones, investment in clean and affordable public transport and incentives for its use, a move back from diesel to petrol or at least a ban on all highly polluting diesel vehicles, lowering speed limits and enhancing cycle routes.

Another intervention in moving towards a cleaner and healthier environment necessitates behavioural changes by the public, which in turn requires continued education and optimal communication. Engagement must be blatant and put in the context of other public health risks such as passive smoking, it must also utilise compelling messages such as premature death. In an ideal world, people, and especially susceptible individuals, should be aware of their air quality by regularly checking the AQI or targeted notifications for real-time data before going to work, school or to pursue leisure activities, enabling them to take action in the event of increased pollution. Improving air quality is a considerable but not an intractable challenge. Translating the correct scientific evidence into bold, realistic and effective policies undisputedly has the potential to reduce air pollution so that it no longer poses a damaging and costly toll on public health.

5

Public Relations Campaigns Can Manipulate Scientific Research

Allan M. Brandt

Allan M. Brandt is part of the department of the history of science and the department of global health and social medicine at Harvard University.

Allan M. Brandt details efforts by the tobacco industry over several decades to subvert and dispute scientific research on the public health impacts of cigarettes and other tobacco products. The effort involved litigation strategies and an extensive public relations campaign. This serves as a paradigmatic example of the ways in which industries can attempt to combat scientific research through public relations campaigns.

[...]

The Tobacco Industry in Crisis Mode

By late 1953, the tobacco industry faced a crisis of cataclysmic proportions. Smoking had been categorically linked to the dramatic rise of lung cancer. Although health concerns about smoking had been raised for decades, by the early 1950s there was a powerful expansion and consolidation of scientific methods and findings that demonstrated that smoking caused lung disease as well as other serious respiratory and cardiac diseases, leading to death. These findings appeared in major,

"Inventing Conflicts of Interest: A History of Tobacco Industry Tactics," by Allan M. Brandt, American Public Health Association, January 2012.

peer-reviewed medical journals as well as throughout the general media.

As a result, the tobacco industry would launch a new strategy, largely unprecedented in the history of US industry and business: it would work to erode, confuse, and condemn the very science that now threatened to destroy its prized, highly popular, and exclusive product. But this would be no simple matter. After all, in the immediate postwar years—the dawn of the nuclear age—science was in high esteem. The industry could not denigrate the scientific enterprise and still maintain its public credibility, so crucial to its success.

The tobacco industry already had a long history of innovative advertising, marketing, and public relations that had centered on making smoking universal. Starting in the late 19th century, the industry transformed itself to become a model of modern industrial organization and consumer marketing. The industry took a product that had existed at the cultural periphery and remade it into one of the most popular, successful, and widely used items of the early 20th century. The basic tenet of the highly articulated public relations approach the companies deployed centered on the notion that if the current cultural context was inhospitable to the product, one could—through shrewd and creative public relations interventions—change the culture to fit the product.

In the course of this transformation, the tobacco companies successfully defined and exploited critical aspects of a new consumer culture. Within the industry, marketing experts had developed a powerful notion of social engineering, what early public relations theorist Edward Bernays had called the "engineering of consent." According to the logic of this approach, society and culture could be manipulated through public relations to create a marketing environment that favored a particular product, in this instance the cigarette. Individuals' purchase of a particular product constituted their consent to the underlying meaning-centered campaigns.

It was this approach to "engineering" that would fundamentally inform the industry's approach to the crisis of the 1950s. After all, if public relations could engineer consent among consumers, so too could it manage the science that was now threatening to undermine the tobacco industry's product and the entire industry itself. And yet, as subsequent history would show, the management of culture and social meaning was considerably different from the management of science.

[...]

Industry Response to Emerging Tobacco Science

By the early 1950s, the emerging science on tobacco's harms documented in the elite peer-reviewed literature, especially the causal linkage to lung cancer, threatened to undo more than a half century of unprecedented corporate success. With considerable anxiety and rancor within the tobacco industry, the industry's highly competitive CEOs came together in December 1953 at the Plaza Hotel in New York City to map a strategy. They realized that the threat they now faced was unprecedented and would require new, collaborative approaches and expertise. Not surprisingly, given their history, they turned again to the field of public relations that had served them so well in the past. They called upon John W. Hill, the president of the nation's leading public relations firm, Hill & Knowlton.

The public confidence the industry required could not be achieved through advertising, which was self-interested by definition. It would be crucial for the industry to assert its authority over the scientific domain; science had the distinct advantage of its reputation for disinterestedness. Hill shared with his public relations predecessor Bernays a deep skepticism about the role of advertising in influencing public perceptions of tobacco. To those schooled in public relations, advertising ran the risk of exposing corporate self-interest. Good public relations relied on scrupulous behind-the-scenes management of media. As Bernays had demonstrated in the 1920s and 1930s, the best public relations work left no fingerprints.

Hill offered the companies powerful advice and guidance as they faced their crisis. Hill understood that simply denying emerging scientific facts would be a losing game. This would not only smack of self-interest but also ally the companies with ignorance in an age of technological and scientific hegemony. So he proposed seizing and controlling science rather than avoiding it. If science posed the principal—even terminal—threat to the industry, Hill advised that the companies should now associate themselves as great supporters of science. The companies, in his view, should embrace a sophisticated scientific discourse; they should demand more science, not less.

Of critical importance, Hill argued, they should declare the positive value of scientific skepticism of science itself. Knowledge, Hill understood, was hard won and uncertain, and there would always be skeptics. What better strategy than to identify, solicit, support, and amplify the views of skeptics of the causal relationship between smoking and disease? Moreover, the liberal disbursement of tobacco industry research funding to academic scientists could draw new skeptics into the fold. The goal, according to Hill, would be to build and broadcast a major scientific controversy. The public must get the message that the issue of the health effects of smoking remains an open question. Doubt, uncertainty, and the truism that there is more to know would become the industry's collective new mantra.

Hill was above all a cynic, deeply committed to the instrumental ideals of public relations. He was profoundly confident that public relations strategies, well developed and implemented, could effectively serve the needs of his clients. He believed—and he convinced the companies' leadership—that by calling for more research and offering funding, they could take high ground in their public pronouncements. Although he had quit smoking himself, he had no interest in examining and assessing the data or the emerging science. For Hill, science would be a means to a public relations end. The executives of the 5 major companies endorsed his strategic plan and hired Hill & Knowlton to manage their burgeoning corporate crisis.

The Tobacco Industry Research Committee

Hill and his colleagues set to work to review the full range of approaches open to them. Dismissing as shortsighted the idea of mounting personal attacks on researchers or simply issuing blanket assurances of safety, they concluded instead that seizing control of the science of tobacco and health would be essential to seizing control of the media. Although public relations practitioners had considerable experience manipulating the media, what was radical about Hill's proposed strategy was the desire to manipulate scientific research, debate, and outcomes. It would be crucial to identify scientists who expressed skepticism about the link between cigarettes and cancer, those critical of statistical methods, and especially those who had offered alternative hypotheses for the causes of cancer.

Hill set his staff to identifying the most vocal and visible skeptics of the emerging science of smoking and disease. These scientists (many of whom turned out to be smokers themselves) would be central to the development of an industry scientific program in step with larger public relations goals. Hill understood that simply denying the harms of smoking would alienate the public. His strategy for ending what the tobacco CEOs called the hysteria linking smoking to cancer was to insist that there were 2 sides in a highly contentious scientific debate. Just as Bernays had worked to engineer consent, so Hill would engineer controversy. This strategy—invented by Hill in the context of his work for the tobacco industry—would ultimately become the cornerstone of a large range of efforts to distort scientific process for commercial ends during the second half of the 20th century.

Individual tobacco companies had sought to compile information that cast doubt on the smoking–cancer connection even before Hill & Knowlton became involved. One R.J. Reynolds official announced to other industry executives in November 1953 that the company had formed a bureau of scientific information to "combat the propaganda which is being directed at the tobacco industry." At the same time, American Tobacco began to collect the public statements of scientists who had expressed skepticism about the research findings indicting tobacco. The company's own public relations counsel understood that it would be critical to create questions about the reliability of the new findings and to attack the notion that these studies constituted proof of the relationship of smoking to cancer.

Pooling these efforts, Hill & Knowlton produced a compendium of statements by physicians and scientists who questioned the cigarette–lung cancer link. This compendium became a fundamental component of Hill & Knowlton's initial attempts to shape and implement its public relations strategy.

After the December 15 meeting that formally brought Hill & Knowlton into the picture, its executives spent the next 2 weeks meeting with various industry staff. During this time, Hill & Knowlton operated in full crisis mode. Executives and staff canceled all holiday plans as they worked to frame and implement a full-scale campaign on behalf of the industry. They made no independent attempt to assess the state of medical knowledge, nor did they seek informed evaluations from independent scientists. Their role was exclusively limited to serving the public relations goal of their collective clients.

During these meetings, both Hill & Knowlton staffers and tobacco executives continued to voice the conviction that the industry's entire future was threatened by the medical and scientific findings linking cigarette smoking to lung cancer and the consequent widespread public anxieties about smoking and health.

> Because of the serious nature of the attack on cigarettes and the vast publicity given them in the daily press and in magazines of the widest circulation, a hysteria of fear appears to be developing throughout the country,

Hill wrote in an internal memorandum. "There is no evidence that this adverse publicity is abating or will soon abate." According to his media intelligence, at least 4 major periodicals (*Look Magazine, Cosmopolitan, Woman's Home Companion,* and *Pageant*) were planning articles on smoking and health.

It was Hill who hit on the idea of creating an industry-sponsored research entity. Ultimately, he concluded, the best public relations approach was for the industry to become a major sponsor of medical research. This tactic offered several essential advantages. The call for new research implied that existing studies were inadequate or flawed. It made clear that there was more to know, and it made the industry seem a committed participant in the scientific enterprise rather than a self-interested critic.

The industry had supported some individual research in recent years, but Hill's proposal offered the potential of a research program that would be controlled by the industry yet promoted as independent. This was a public relations masterstroke. Hill understood that simply giving money to scientists—through the National Institutes of Health or some other entity, for example—offered little opportunity to shape the public relations environment. However, offering funds directly to university-based scientists would enlist their support and dependence. Moreover, it would have the added benefit of making academic institutions "partners" with the tobacco industry in its moment of crisis.

The very nature of controlling and managing information in public relations stood in marked contrast to the scientific notion of unfettered new knowledge. Hill and his clients had no interest in answering a scientific question. Their goal was to maintain vigorous control over the research program, to use science in the service of public relations. Although the tobacco executives had proposed forming a cigarette information committee dedicated to defending smoking against the medical findings, Hill argued aggressively for adding research to the committee's title and agenda. "It is believed," he wrote, "that the word 'Research' is needed in the name to give weight and added credence to the Committee's statements." Hill understood that his clients should be viewed as embracing science rather than dismissing it.

Hill also advised the industry that continued competitive assertions about the health benefits of particular brands would be devastating. Instead, the industry needed a collective research initiative to demonstrate its shared concern for the public. Rather than using health research to create competitive products as they had been doing, the companies needed to express—above all else—their commitment to public well-being. Hill believed that the competitive fervor over health claims had harmed the industry's credibility. No one would look for serious information about health from an industry that was making unsubstantiated claims about its product.

The future of the industry would reflect its acceptance of this essential principle. From December 1953 forward, the tobacco companies would present a unified front on smoking and health; more than 5 decades of strategic and explicit collusion would follow. The Tobacco Industry Research Committee (TIRC), a group that would be carefully shaped by Hill & Knowlton to serve the industry's collective interests, would be central to the explicit goal of controlling the scientific discourse about smoking and health. The public announcement of the formation of the committee came in a full-page advertisement run in more than 400 newspapers across the country, soon known as the "frank statement." The ad promised that the companies would aggressively pursue the science of tobacco and ensure the well-being of their consumers:

> We accept an interest in people's health as a basic responsibility, paramount to every other consideration in our business. We believe the products we make are not injurious to health. We always have and always will cooperate closely with those whose task it is to safeguard the public health.

The frank statement remains a powerful illustration of how Hill was prepared to use science in the interest of his clients. It is a model of the "new" public relations that he established at midcentury.

Hill carefully outlined the plans for a research program before a single scientist was consulted. The utility of such a strategy was its apparent commitment to objective science and its search for the truth. As one colleague argued,

A flamboyant campaign against the anti-smoking propagandists would unquestionably alienate much of the support of the moderates in both scientific and lay publics.

Instead, tobacco companies had to respect the moral valence of science in American culture at midcentury. If science now threatened the industry, the industry must "secure" science.

The TIRC, from its inception, was dominated by its public relations goals. Alton Ochsner, the well-known thoracic surgeon who had conducted research on the relationship of smoking to heart disease, saw his own hopes for funding support from the industry fade as the TIRC's research agenda quickly became clear. He noted,

Of course, the critical areas of investigation, as every research scientist knows, have to do with the problem of how to make smoking a less lethal agent in lung cancer incidence and a less deadly killer in heart disease.... Yet it is precisely these areas that apparently have been declared out of bounds for the industry's research committee.

Internal industry assessments confirmed Ochsner's view. As one internal industry evaluation would conclude a decade later, "most of the TIRC research has been of a broad, basic nature not designed to specifically test the anti-cigarette theory." From the outset, Hill & Knowlton exerted full control over the industry's collaborative research program. The TIRC administrative offices were even located at Hill & Knowlton's New York office. W.T. Hoyt, executive director of the TIRC, came to the position with no scientific experience whatsoever. Before joining Hill & Knowlton, he sold advertising for the *Saturday Evening Post*. At Hill & Knowlton, where he began work in 1951, he had run the iron and steel industry's Scrap Mobilization Committee. In early 1954, he assumed a dominant role in the day-to-day operations of the tobacco industry research program. Ultimately, Hoyt would become a full-time employee, remaining integral to the TIRC until he retired in 1984.

Tobacco company leaders also played important roles in the organization. In the early months of operation, Paul Hahn of American Tobacco and Parker McComas of Philip Morris served as its acting chairs. The first full-time chairman of TIRC was Timothy Hartnett, the retired CEO of Brown & Williamson. The press release announcing his appointment read, in part, as follows:

> It is an obligation of the Tobacco Industry Research Committee at this time to remind the public of these essential points:
> There is no conclusive scientific proof of a link between smoking and cancer.
> Medical research points to many possible causes of cancer.... .
> The millions of people who derive pleasure and satisfaction from smoking can be reassured that every scientific means will be used to get all the facts as soon as possible.

Hartnett and his successors would reiterate this message for the next 40 years.

[...]

6

Manufacturers Can Produce Misleading Scientific Research to Protect Themselves

Union of Concerned Scientists

The Union of Concerned Scientists is a nonprofit science advocacy organization based in the United States.

This viewpoint looks at the case of the manufacturer Georgia-Pacific, which produced misleading scientific research reports to shield the company from liability or regulatory action related to a joint compound that contained asbestos. Their use of counterfeit science demonstrates the ways in which people depend on scientific research to properly comprehend the hazards they face at home and in the workplace, as well as how falsified scientific reports can put the public in danger.

I n an attempt to reduce litigation costs, Georgia-Pacific launched a secret campaign to produce and publish counterfeit science designed to raise doubts about the dangers of asbestos.

What Happened

From the turn of the century through the 1970s, asbestos was inescapable. The so-called "magic mineral" was in fireproof theater curtains, gas masks, prison-cell padding, brake linings, and thousands of other products.

One such product—a version of the construction material known as joint compound, sold under the name Ready-Mix—

"How Georgia-Pacific Knowingly Published Fake Science on the Safety of Asbestos," Union of Concerned Scientists. Reprinted by permission.

contained asbestos from 1965 to 1977 and proved to be a major problem for its manufacturer Georgia-Pacific, a conglomerate now owned by Koch Industries that specializes in wood and paper products. As the dangers from asbestos became publicly known, Georgia-Pacific, like many other companies that had made asbestos-containing products, became swamped with a deluge of legal claims from people who had contracted lung disease from exposure to the company's product.

Rather than face those claims honestly, beginning in 2005, Georgia-Pacific crafted and published *counterfeit science*—seeding the literature with articles intended to raise doubts about the dangers posed by asbestos. In so doing, the company created a life-threatening hazard by deceiving those who rely on science to understand the health risks of asbestos exposure.

Asbestos—which is not a single mineral at all, but rather a collective name for six fibrous minerals—has been shown by many scientific studies to be extremely dangerous to human health. Both domestic and international government agencies now classify it as a known human carcinogen, linked to asbestosis, mesothelioma, and other lung cancers. Since the 1970s, its use has been heavily regulated, although it is not banned in the US.

In 1977, as the Consumer Product Safety Commission (CPSC) moved to ban asbestos-containing joint compound, Georgia-Pacific's chairman even wrote to CPSC that "We support a total ban on spackling compound containing asbestos," as Georgia-Pacific had already "ceased using asbestos in our product and switched to a substitute." Despite that public statement, however, the company privately worried about its liability for having sold the asbestos-containing product for many years.

By 2002, concern about asbestos-related legal claims had severely damaged Georgia-Pacific's stock. An unflattering three-part series in the *Atlanta Journal-Constitution* that year revealed that Georgia-Pacific was aware of the science showing the dangers of asbestos for several years before the company put a warning label on Ready-Mix. The newspaper series caused Georgia-

Pacific's chairman to pen an op-ed in the same paper, claiming that "throughout the years we've dealt with the legal consequences of asbestos fibers, we have worked diligently and in good faith to resolve a staggering 250,000 individual legal claims," and that "we have consistently acted responsibly—for victims, our employees and shareholders."

Even if the company did act as it claimed up to 2002, by 2005—under the guidance of the same chairman—Georgia-Pacific had turned to counterfeit science to fend off lawsuits. That year, the company created a so-called research program—run through its legal department—that knowingly produced flawed science and published it in independent scientific journals while failing to adequately disclose the authors' conflicts of interest.

Documents later obtained by the Center for Public Integrity revealed that Georgia-Pacific put its research strategy into action by hiring its head of toxicology, Stewart Holm, for a "separate and distinct" role as a so-called "litigation consultant." Routing Holm's new work through the legal department allowed the company to claim attorney-client privilege over all documents related to his counterfeit science work, thereby keeping it from the public—a tactic pioneered by the tobacco industry when it conducted counterfeit research to confuse the public about the dangers of cigarettes.

With the counterfeit science program tucked away in its legal department, Georgia-Pacific published 13 scientific articles that were deeply flawed, both in methodology—for instance, opting for a five-day study rather than the preferred two-year study to test whether chronic inhalation of fibers can cause cancers, fibrosis, or mesothelioma—and by not adequately revealing the authors' clear conflicts of interest. None of the papers published through this scheme, for example, disclosed that Georgia-Pacific's legal team had been overseeing almost every aspect of the research.

A multi-year legal battle over internal documents about Georgia-Pacific's research program culminated in a unanimous ruling against the company in June 2013. A New York state appeals court affirmed a trial court's ruling that the company must turn over the documents so that the court could determine whether Georgia-Pacific's actions over the research program were in furtherance of fraud and therefore not covered by attorney-client privilege. The court found ample evidence that Georgia-Pacific's actions could have been in furtherance of fraud, including the company's failure to disclose that its in-house lawyer had reviewed the manuscripts before submission, or that Holm had been concurrently employed with the company for asbestos litigation purposes.

Why It Matters

As this case shows, intentionally publishing counterfeit science endangers public health. People rely on scientific literature to understand the hazards they face at work, at home, and anywhere else. When companies create and publish knowingly flawed science, or even when they fail to disclose important (and in most cases, required) conflicts of interest to journals, the public pays the price. Sometimes, as in this case, matters of life and death are at stake.

Asbestos is especially notable because of how dangerous it is to human health. As noted by the Occupational Health and Safety Administration, "Breathing asbestos fibers can cause a buildup of scar-like tissue in the lungs called asbestosis and result in loss of lung function that often progresses to disability and death. Asbestos also causes cancer of the lung and other diseases such as mesothelioma of the pleura which is a fatal malignant tumor of the membrane lining the cavity of the lung or stomach." Thousands of Americans die every year because of asbestos exposure.

Counterfeit science about asbestos is also particularly damaging because it took many years for the public to fully recognize the dangers of asbestos that scientists were uncovering. Documents released in lawsuits in the 1970s show that major manufacturers knew about the dangers of asbestos as early as the 1930s, but ignored, buried, or silenced scientists and science that could have publicly brought forth the information to the public. Indeed, it took until 1964 for research about the dangers of asbestos to make waves publicly, forcing companies to change their ways and the government to regulate asbestos. And the author of that pioneering science published in 1964—Dr. Irving Selikoff—faced scrutiny and harassment from the asbestos industry.

The question remains: how much safer would the public be if industry had listened to the science in the first place, and if unscrupulous companies such as Georgia-Pacific had not devoted years and resources to undermining the scientific understanding of asbestos with counterfeit science?

7

How Policymakers Can Adapt to Climate Change

Rob Swart, Tiago Capela Lourenco, and Robbert Biesbroek

Rob Swart is a climate scientist at Alterra in the Netherlands. Tiago Capela Lourenço is a climate scientist at the University of Lisbon in Portugal. Robbert Biesbroek is a climate scientist at Wageningen University & Research in the Netherlands.

The authors analyze the strategies and variables related to the effectiveness of international cooperation on climate change research. The viewpoint focuses on efforts among policymakers at different levels of government to adapt to the consequences of climate change. Failure to adapt to climate change is an issue that would impact the entire global population, and as such cooperation in efforts to adapt and curb climate change must be made at an international level. The authors call for a synthesis of "science for adaptation"—or science intended to respond to climate change—and "science of adaptation"—science meant to better understand how climate change works—to most effectively combat it.

A daptation to climate change has gained a prominent place next to mitigation on global, national, and local policy agendas. However, while an abundance of adaptation strategies, plans, and programmes have been developed, progress in turning these into action has been slow. The development of a sound knowledge basis to support adaptation globally is suggested to accelerate progress, but has lagged behind. The emphasis in both current and newly proposed programmes is very much on practice-oriented research with strong stakeholder participation. This paper supports such practice-oriented research, but argues that this is insufficient to support adaptation policy and practice in a productive manner. We argue that there is not only a need for science *for* adaptation, but also a science *of* adaptation. The paper argues that participatory, practice-oriented research is indeed essential, but has to be complemented by and connected to more fundamental inquiry and concept development, which takes into account knowledge that has been developed in disciplinary sciences and on issues other than climate change adaptation. At the same time, the level and method of participation in science for adaptation should be determined on the basis of the specific project context and goals. More emphasis on science of adaptation can lead to improved understanding of the conditions for successful science for adaptation.

Introduction

Ever since the perceived taboo on adaptation to climate change has been lifted (Pielke et al., 2007), adaptation has become politically accepted and institutionalized at different levels of governance: for example, through the establishment of financial instruments at the global level of the United Nations Framework Convention on Climate Change (UNFCCC), the European Union's Climate Change Adaptation Strategy, the increasing number of National Climate Change Adaptation Strategies and plans, and the numerous local and regional initiatives to plan for future climate change risks (Biesbroek et al., 2010; Dreyfus and Patt, 2012). Many examples of adaptation have been reported and now serve as an inspiration for future adaptation efforts across the globe. Still, the World Economic Forum considers the failure to adapt to climate change to be one of the major threats that society faces in the coming decades (WEF, 2013, 2014), requiring even more adaptation action.

In parallel to the policy progress, scientific endeavors on understanding different dimensions of adaptation to climate change and the number of scholarly papers has increased substantially in recent years (Berrang-Ford et al., 2011). The recently published 5th Assessment report of IPCC Working Group II is the most recent assessment of the scientific progress on adaptation. Where previous research has explored the impacts and vulnerabilities of climate risks, recent emphasis in adaptation research programmes, globally, and in Europe, has been on responses, in particular on the softer kind of measures such as capacity building, management, and planning, awareness raising and supply of information, but less on actually changing practices, green or gray infrastructure, or measurable decrease of vulnerability (EEA, 2013; Biagini et al., 2014). Moss et al. (2013) argue that inadequate knowledge for adaptation forms one important reason why progress in delivering adaptation action has been limited. Research to support adaptation therefore needs to move toward other forms of research that better connects to the societal needs (Moser, 2010; O'Brien, 2012; Deppisch and Hasibovic, 2013). Conventional disciplinary approaches are considered to be insufficiently equipped to deal with the intricately connected and inherently wicked nature of climate change risks in a holistic way (ISSC/UNESCO, 2013). A multidisciplinary or interdisciplinary approach, where disciplinary knowledge is, respectively, exchanged or integrated, is deemed necessary but not sufficient to tackle these societally relevant problems either.

The inability to connect the sciences meaningfully with societal needs has been central to different academic disciplines and philosophy of science (Nowotny et al., 2001) and recently entered the discussion on climate change adaptation (see amongst others Moser and Boykoff, 2013) and its connections with climate risk management approaches (IPCC, 2012), namely those that aim at combining adaptation and disaster risk reduction processes. It is argued that future research on climate change adaptation would require the involvement of non-scientific stakeholders in the research enterprise so as to co-define societally relevant problems, to co-produce or co-create relevant knowledge, and to co-learn from these experiences, which in this paper, we consider to be captured by the term "transdisciplinary" (Mauser et al., 2013; Rice, 2013). The term "transdisciplinary" is defined differently in different contexts and its meaning has evolved over time. Defining characteristics are usually problem focus, evolving methodology, and collaboration, with a different balance in different contexts (Wickson et al., 2006; Russell et al., 2008). Nowotny et al. (2001) refer to "knowledge production that is problem-oriented, responsive and open to external knowledge producers, contextualized, and systems-based, adaptable, consultative and socially robust." As we observe in the next section, the involvement of external knowledge producers is typical for the definition used in climate change adaptation programming. So, in this paper we explicitly refer to kinds of transdisciplinary research that does create knowledge beyond disciplinary borders and does also involve stakeholders. The ontological questions of what constitutes a transdisciplinary approach, how it originated, and how its success can be evaluated is beyond the scope of this article (Pohl, 2008, 2011). Yet one defining characteristic, namely problem orientation through a participatory approach is central to this paper. It has been argued that transdisciplinary research is particularly relevant when knowledge is uncertain, the nature of the problem disputed and the consequences of the problem affect large parts of society (Hirsch Hadorn et al., 2007). Although the precise onset of this movement in the recent past remains difficult to identify in time, we observe that the scientific discourse on adaptation seems to move in the direction of one unified, practice-oriented, transdisciplinary form of science aiming to inform "decision makers," even though it is often unclear who exactly these decision makers are or which precise questions they have. This movement can be regarded as part of a broader trend which Bäckstrand et al. (2010) labeled the deliberative turn in environmental governance. Although there can be no objection against socially relevant research on adaptation, we feel that there are some critical reflections and nuances currently missing in the debates on the future of adaptation research, which we will discuss in this paper.

First, we review some of the key elements of current and proposed adaptation research programmes related to practice-oriented research and identify their strengths and weaknesses— which we call the science *for* adaptation. Then we focus on the need for—and early efforts on—a science *of* adaptation. Finally, we discuss a number of future directions that this research can take to build both a science *for* and *of* adaptation, and connections between them.

[…]

Science for Adaptation: Practice-Oriented Research and Bridging the Science-Policy-Practice Divide

The research programmes above demonstrate considerable efforts in practice-oriented research on adaptation. However, one could pose the question if it would be justified to develop a distinct, novel "adaptation science" to support adaptation, or if adaptation is mainly an act of practice, one that can be studied using multiple scientific perspectives. This question is yet to be answered. Some have argued that there are at least some signs of such an emerging "adaptation science." According to Moss et al. (2013), adaptation science is at best still in a formative stage.

Moss et al. (2013) provide a comprehensive proposal for the development of an integrated and practice-relevant adaptation science, to understand decision processes and knowledge requirements, identify vulnerabilities, improve foresight about climate risks and other stressors, and understand barriers and options for adaptation (Moss et al., 2013). Practice-oriented or socially relevant research is unquestionably of utmost importance, and is justified for many societal challenges, including adaptation. However, to what extent does transdisciplinary research indeed lead to societal impacts, e.g., in terms of decreased vulnerability to climate change? More co-produced knowledge is often assumed to lead to more and better adaptation because of tangible connections between the research and social needs and interests (Hegger et al., 2012). But is this really true? An evaluation of the societal impact of the two Dutch climate change research programmes suggests that the impact has been greatest on agenda setting (Merkx et al., 2012). Knowledge on climate change amongst societal actors has been increased, the magnitude, and diversity of networks have been improved, tools have been developed that are also used by actors not involved in the programme, and knowledge has effectively been co-created. However, with a few exceptions, these positive outcomes have generally not led to actual implementation of adaptation actions, and the durability of the impacts is uncertain (Merkx et al., 2012).

[...]

Science of Adaptation: Search for Disciplinary Pluralism

As discussed above, the science *for* adaptation evolves mainly in a transdisciplinary fashion, by analyzing how to address societal adaptation challenges in various real-word contexts using available theories and data to describe and advise policy practice. We postulate that good policy recommendations require linkages between science, policy, and society, but it also requires reflexive distance and scientific evidence to support the advice on how to best adapt to climate change. There are obviously potentially intractable conflicts between the aims of the science *of* adaptation (to better understand) and the science *for* adaptation (to support policy and practice), but too much focus on the science *for* adaptation would be problematic since in the end it should be to a large extent dependent on the science *of* adaptation. The questions posed in the latter might not be immediately socially relevant, but they are necessary to inform meaningful science *for* adaptation. A science *of* adaptation would approach adaptation to climate change as an observable societal act that can be studied from different angles and adopting different disciplinary perspectives, grounded in and requiring expertise from the forefront of both natural and social disciplinary sciences, to really understand some of the fundamental aspects of the adaptation. The context of this paper we specifically imply social science disciplines which have been underrepresented in adaptation research to date. One example is the (*a priori*) need to embark in stakeholder engagement or co-creation processes as a fundamental step in moving adaptation practice. A science *of* adaptation can point out if there are recurring patterns and processes in stakeholder involvement across cases that can determine under which conditions certain types of stakeholder involvement is proven to be most effective to implement measures to adapt, or suggest conditions where no or limited participation is perhaps more effective (see for example Few et al., 2007).

[…]

Connecting Science of and Science for Adaptation: A Diversified Approach

In this paper, we noted the tendency in current and programmed research on climate change adaptation to move toward a single, transdisciplinary approach with a strong co-production and stakeholder involvement component. We call this the science *for* adaptation. Patt (2013) raised the question: "what if adaptation isn't really a very good science of its own"? We argue that, alone, the current science for adaptation may not really meet the standard of "a very good science of its own." Furthermore, and considering the importance of adaptation as one of the most pressing societal issues (WEF, 2013, 2014), we do believe it can also be scientifically strengthened. We therefore plea for a scientific endeavor that captures and balances both science for and of adaptation. Whether this combination should be called "adaptation science" may not be a very meaningful question from a purely scientific perspective.

It may be of practical and linguistic interest, for example when developing specific (new) journals, in the design of academic courses and research programmes, financing disciplinary research projects of adaptation, or even the development of new academic or other institutions.

Rather than suggesting to develop a "science of adaptation" research line in parallel to the current science for adaptation, we here more modestly suggest to correct the growing bias in the current adaptation research programmes and funding schemes toward a better balance between science *for* and *of* adaptation. This would recognize that some distance between these two types of research is needed for reflection, synthesis, and further learning. While we acknowledge that learning by doing in participatory, practice-oriented research is useful and can be productive, we also argue that a better understanding of the underlying theoretical frames and processes can lead to a more effective support to decision-making processes on the longer-term; it is too soon to only focus on transdisciplinary and practice-oriented research. Here, we refer to social science questions about what exactly does adaptation entail, both theoretically and conceptually, enhancing an understanding that may be as—or even more- important than improvements in climate modeling or impact studies for advancing climate change adaptation in practice.

Strengthening the science for adaptation requires overcoming a number of barriers created by the move toward transdisciplinary research and how the research on adaptation has evolved: (1) application of untested heuristics in practice; (2) scientists as problem-solvers; (3) confusion about framing and terminology; (4) unattractiveness for disciplinary researchers, and (5) one-size-fits-all approaches. In particular, we feel that the idea of the transdisciplinary research endeavor will not be sufficiently attractive to involve the disciplinary social sciences. A better understanding is required of the types of knowledge that are needed to support the science for adaptation which, in turn, allow to allocate scientific research funding to disciplinary focussed research projects that may not be of immediate societal relevance. In particular, we propose to give more weight in climate change adaptation research to science of adaptation that would encourage to (1) break through heuristics and clarify key concepts; (2) move toward testing and explanatory ambitions, and (3) allow for multiplicity of ontological perspectives and methodological variety.

A new generation of scholars on climate change adaptation might be able to connect across scientific disciplines, be sensitive to practice-relevant questions, to couple science and practice, and to provide clear and simple stories (Mustelin et al., 2013). They are an integral component for the success of the practice-oriented research endeavor. We envision an important share of the new generation of scholars on climate change adaptation to be generalists, educated to assist addressing real world problems. But this means that there is also an increasing need for a science *of* adaptation—to provide substantive insights and recommendations to support transdisciplinary research. This combination of disciplinary, interdisciplinary, and transdisciplinary research would encourage a broader spectrum of relevant disciplinary sciences to become involved in adaptation science beyond just a transdisciplinary, practice-oriented approach.

If research funding and programming agencies would aim to strike a good balance between a science *for* adaptation and a science *of* adaptation, the societal impacts can be much larger than a sole focus on practice-oriented science, which may lead to a million case studies without necessarily a good understanding of underlying processes or the development of appropriate frameworks and methodologies. We hope that in the new Interdisciplinary Climate Studies journal of Frontiers in Environmental Science there will be room for both a science *for* adaptation and a science *of* adaptation.

8

The Nature and Politics of Scientific Debates in America

Adi Melamed

Adi Melamed is a community organizer and a writer at the Brown Political Review.

This viewpoint explores why scientific issues have such an emotional register in American political discourse, and why public opinion on scientific matters can differ from the consensus within the scientific community. The climate change debate in America serves as a key example of this tendency. Melamed argues that this is partly due to the conflicted nature of the relationship between scientists and the general public.

The 2016 Presidential debates were fraught with insults, drama, and disparaging comments. To the dismay of many, though, they were completely devoid of any discussion of climate change. The issue of climate change continued to be tossed aside as Donald Trump derided its existence, importance, and impact. Once elected, Trump appointed Myron Ebell, an outspoken climate change denier, to lead the transition team for the Environmental Protection Agency. And finally, in February, Scott Pruitt — another climate change denier — was confirmed as the head of the Environmental Protection Agency.

"The Attitudes, Rhetoric, and Politics of Scientific Debate," by Adi Melamed, Brown Political Review, March 11, 2017. Reprinted by permission. Originally published by Adi Melamed in The Brown Political Review.

The fight against and denial of climate change is not a new issue. Since the 1990s, climate change has been debated as a political issue, with the first contrarian scientists such as Frederick Seitz coming out against the established scientific consensus. While it is common in the history of science for scientific theories to initially be rejected by public authorities or public opinion, it is still noteworthy that as of 2016, 36 percent of American adults do not worry about climate change, and 57 percent of American adults do not perceive climate change as a serious threat. And climate change is not alone in the uphill battle for recognition. The theories, effects, and validity of scientific thought on evolution, vaccines, cigarettes, and gender are all rejected and denied by portions of the American public. Why do debates of scientific matters rage on? Why is it, that even when well over 90 percent of climate change scientists are in agreement about man-made climate change, the American public is still reluctant to acknowledge its existence?

On one level, it is because like all matters, science is inherently political. Matters of politics must be fought for, negotiated, and debated. Just because scientists come to a consensus does not mean that all political groups will immediately accept it. Similarly, the science of climate change has political implications at odds with interest groups such as the oil industry, economic implications at odds with interest groups such as free-market libertarians, and "legitimacy" implications at odds with groups that endorse the word of religious institutions.

Most importantly, the scientific community's attempt to characterize scientific knowledge as objective, as a pillar of truth not to be questioned by the public, creates a conflictual relationship between the "authority" and the "subject," the scientists and the public. Just as there has been a rise in the "reclamation" of American government from the "establishment-swamp" by populists, so, too, has there been a reclamatory movement against scientists as bearers of truth. If scientists wish to maintain their authority and influence as conveyors of scientific and objective knowledge, they must meet the public on the battlegrounds and respond with rhetoric that the public understands. Scientists must be both scientific and political — both authority figures and members of our communities.

In presenting the issue of climate change to the public, scientists face fierce opposition. Oil companies, conservative scientists, and free market libertarians fight together and rally against a scientific consensus on climate change. Like all other groups, it is in their interest to preserve and maximize their political and economic interests. And this is exactly what they've done. An in-depth piece by Philip Kitcher in "Science" reports on an important study carried out by historians Naomi Oreskes and Erik M. Conway, which argues that a small number of scientists have opposed well-supported claims, including those about the dangers of cigarette smoking and climate change, to protect corporate, political, and commercial interests. There are a relatively small number of these obfuscators who play a disproportionate role in such discussions, even though many are trained in fields not pertinent to the issues up for debate. Kitcher writes, "[T]hey have been able to cast enough doubt on the consensus views arrived at by scientists within the relevant disciplines to delay, often for a substantial period, widespread public acceptance of consequential hypotheses."

Climate change deniers work under the veneer of scientific rhetoric by providing an "alternate view." By co-opting scientific rhetoric, they can work under the appearance of scientific legitimacy that fails only under close scrutiny. The problem is that, for those who lean politically or economically conservative, there is no incentive to look at the climate change debate with close scrutiny. Several studies have shown that the greatest indicator of someone's belief on climate change is their political affiliation. It is well known that confirmation bias is ubiquitous, penetrating what we choose to believe and what evidence will refute without second consideration. Unfortunately, psychologists have repeatedly discovered that those who are misinformed and later corrected often lapse into versions of their original error; this leads some to say it may be less important to change people's minds in the first place, than it is to mobilize environmentalist voters and representatives to action.

Coupled with the media's tendency to portray the climate change discussion as "still up for debate" by presenting two sides, or to ensure that they have "balanced coverage," it is not surprising that the fight for the acceptance of man-made climate change has been so difficult. That being said, climate change scientists haven't always responded to these issues well. James Hansen of Columbia University and the late Stephen Schneider of Stanford University spent 30 years alerting policymakers, politicians, and the public to the dangers of climate change — and were met with frustrating obstacles and unfulfilling success. Kitcher says, "Their experiences incline them to emphasize the importance of expert judgment, effectively renewing the ancient worries about the dangers of democracy. Both believe that genuine democratic participation in the issues can only begin when citizens are in a position to understand what kinds of policies promote their interests." Other climate scientists, though, such as Mike Hulme of the UK, "chide" Hansen and Schneider for what he believes are overly "apocalyptic pronouncements" about climate change. To Hansen and Schneider's credit, they certainly have good intention and have been rebutting the same "alternative views" for decades.

At the heart of the matter is how scientists should respond to the pushback from political and corporate groups that would be harmed by environmental regulation. The success of climate change deniers lends credence to a rhetorical approach that meshes politics with science — and recognizes the political interests behind the whole debate. Lynda Walsh, in the "Wiley Journal for Climate Change," effectively frames this argument, claiming that scientists' attempts to make climate change about "science not rhetoric" ignore the irrational aspects of how humans process information, are ignorant of the power of rhetoric to persuade an audience, and pretend that science can be divorced from politics, thereby stalling effective political action. A study published by two professors from Australia and Hong Kong demonstrated that rhetoric could bridge the gap between an environmentalist and a group of climate change deniers to bring the deniers into accepting "particular greenhouse gas mitigation measures" as acceptable policy choices. Scientists, then, might be able to avoid the elitist derision of democracy, if they change their rhetoric to be about more than rational discourse. Ultimately, it is not that the public is "stupid," but rather that most arguments are won on more than reason, whether we like that or not.

It should become apparent then that while scientists are, and should be, the ultimate authority on scientific knowledge, there is a danger in expressing scientific consensus to the public with that kind of hubris. There is a difference, for example, between recognizing that a healthy democracy requires a "division of labor" on political and public matters so that experts can share consensus views, and in diminishing public opinion as unimportant, stupid, or unresponsive to logic. The lesson the scientific community should take from the 2016 election is not that the American public is not concerned about climate change (mostly because that was already obvious), but more so that the American public is expressing a latent resentment to authority and establishment politics, won over by simple rhetoric.

If the scientific community does not want to be swept up with the rest of the "swamp," it is best for them to realize that expert judgment doesn't mean public derision. Rational discourse can be accompanied by political rhetoric. The public sphere is inherently political, so the debate that scientists must take on is political. Recognizing this could give scientists the tools to strengthen the scientific-political coalition that rallies behind the scientific enterprise. It is unfortunate and unfair that well-intentioned scientists face such a skeptical (though the denialist term, "politically polarized" is more fitting) American public. Science, the scientific consensus, and the authority of scientists merit respect, but it is more productive that scientists be better equipped against corporate groups obfuscating the climate change debate than it is to remain true to the ideals of "experts-only, rationality-only" discourse.

9

The Difference Between Science and Politics

Michael Tobis

Michael Tobis holds a PhD in atmospheric and oceanic science from the University of Wisconsin-Madison. He is also a software developer and the editor-in-chief of Planet3.0.

In this viewpoint, Michael Tobis asserts that the political sphere is an intellectual dead zone characterized by manipulation, misleading language, and motivated reasoning. He also contrasts this to the particular features of scientific discourse that allow it to grow progressively. He characterizes science as fundamentally different from politics in that science is about slow and steady progress rather than grand theatrical gestures with little actual impact, which is what Tobis asserts politics involves.

There was once a minor low budget panel program on television somewhere, I can't recall where, perhaps it was PBS, perhaps the CBC, called "This Week in Science" or something to that effect. I guess it had responded to demands from the public for more science news. The panel all seemed to be journalists of some middling TV-safe stripe or other. You know, not stupid but somehow reliably noncontroversial just the same. (To my way of seeing things this is a very odd form of intelligence.)

And to see this crowd discussing the week's events in science was comically lame, because from their point of view, what

"The Main Difference Between Science and Politics," by Michael Tobis, planet3.org, November 29, 2011. Reprinted by permission.

happened in science in the previous week was *precisely and exactly nothing*. Essentially nothing changes in science from week to week. Nothing of any importance occurs that changes the scene from one week to the next. Occasionally a major study is released, of course, but everybody interested in the topic already knows what it will say by the time it is published.

Compare this to what happens in politics. The strutting, the striving, the gaffes, the bons mots, the triumphs, the tragedies, the legislative victories, the judicial defeats, the tarnishing of old heroes, the vindication of villains, the arrival of fresh new warriors… It's positively Shakespearean.

Yet come back ten years later.

The politicians, with some shifts in dramatis personae, will be making almost exactly the same bleats and whinnies in almost exactly the same order. The problems will be the same, perhaps slightly changed in emphasis. The disagreements on what to value will be the same. Perhaps the disagreements on actual, substantive facts will have worsened. Perhaps the choices of which facts are salient will have even further diverged.

Meanwhile the scientists will be discussing completely different things, most of their questions from a decade ago having been addressed to general satisfaction!

How is this possible?

It is possible because science *learns*. There is *a consistent direction* to it. It always marches, slowly, ponderously, but steadily onward to deeper understanding. It rarely backtracks, and almost never on matters of importance.

Politics is almost impervious to learning.

And once a scientific field gets swallowed up by politics, it gets a strange double character. Within its core, it continues to make progress, but at its fringes, the progress is successfully concealed, obfuscated by people who will never get the point of anything. A spectacular example is the recent raising of the DeFreitas/Baliunas/Soon vs von Storch et al fiasco by Anthony Watts. This is one of the most embarrassing incidents in the history of denialism, wherein

Hans von Storch, a genuine skeptic about the urgency of climate change, was considered reliable enough to be the editor of a journal which was intended to whitewash denialist nonsense of the sort that Soon and Baliunas have been peddling for some considerable time. Von Storch was having none of it, and after some argument, resigned as editor and convinced much of the rest of the board to leave with him.

Now the Baliunas & Soon paper is a good example of "postnormal" process in science. Their purpose was not to get a robust result in press. *Their purpose was to get a result, no matter how dubious, which was embarrassing to the consensus into print, so that they could trumpet it to a senate committee.* Which they proceeded to do.

Now stolen emails reveal considerable discomfort among actual scientists about this. But the end result was enormously embarrassing to the perpetrators. Furthermore, although clearly von Storch wants to put the matter behind him and get back to the more entertaining business of genuine disagreement with the consensus, he is still around to testify to the inadequate nature of Baliunas & Soon's work and de Freitas's editorial judgment if pressed. Why on earth would Watts want to bring this up again?

Because in politics no victory need ever be conceded. After enough time passes, a new garbling of the story can be proposed to advance the cause. *Nothing is ever settled.* Despite von Storch's vigorous and repeated assertions that nobody pressured him and that he was simply defending the quality of science, sinister implications can be drummed up, *waters can be muddied, progress can be prevented.*

It is into this dreadful context that we find ourselves injected if we have the misfortune of making a discovery with consequences for governance. And here we are presented with bounties of stupid advice, advice that is appropriate for the day to day battles of groups that expect to make no progress, to battle to an endless dysfunctional stalemate, to win some and lose some.

What we need is a politics that makes progress. What we need is a way to build a social contract. What we need is a politics of consensus.

In the climate change matter, it is of vanishingly small consequence if the Democrats prevail in 2012, for their opponents will surely prevail in 2014 or 2016 or 2018 or 2020. *What we need is to win over their opponents*, so that we proceed from a social consensus. And indeed, we need a consensus that is not merely national but global.

The talks at Durban are a charade. The COPs will continue their charade-like existence until the world understands our predicament and swallows the obviously needed medicine. What happens in the Republican party or the Democratic party, or comparable organizations elsewhere, is of modest consequence. The only hope is in what happens in the minds of the voters; *all of them.*

There is no feasible alternative to the smokescreen of denial other than a deliberate and clear presentation of reality in a way that is, if possible, encouraging and life-affirming and liberating, but regardless of sales techniques, is actually true.

Without reviving a shared vision of progress to a brighter future we can only attain more atrophy and more acrimony and more decay.

Progress no longer means more and more and more stuff. But it can be progress toward a brighter and more humane future just the same. The solution to our woes is not that science should become more like politics, but the other way around.

10

The Fossil Fuel Industry Is Using Obstruction and Deception to Fight the EPA

Union of Concerned Scientists

The Union of Concerned Scientists is a nonprofit science advocacy organization based in the United States.

This viewpoint examines how research backed by the fossil fuel industry has been used in lobbying and public relations to push back against the Environmental Protection Agency's (EPA) efforts to regulate carbon pollution, which the industry views as a threat. It discusses various methods companies in the fossil fuels and utilities industries use to obstruct the EPA's ability to take action on climate change. However, the author argues that increased public awareness will help prevent fossil fuels and utilities companies from further obstructing the EPA's ability to monitor and combat climate change.

On February 9, 2016, the Supreme Court placed a hold on the Environmental Protection Agency's (EPA's) Clean Power Plan, the first-ever limits on heat-trapping carbon dioxide pollution from power plants. It's the latest development in a disinformation campaign perpetrated by fossil fuel and utility interests to stop EPA action on climate change.

It's a story that goes back for years. In 1998, amidst Congressional gridlock on climate change, the EPA asserted its legal authority to regulate carbon pollution under existing

"Who's Fighting the Clean Power Plan and EPA Action on Climate Change?" Union of Concerned Scientists. Reprinted by permission.

provisions of the Clean Air Act. A memorandum from the EPA's General Counsel affirmed that the agency had the authority to regulate carbon pollution, so long as it first found heat-trapping emissions that contribute to climate change could endanger public health and welfare or the environment. Nine years later, in 2007, the Supreme Court agreed.

In 2009, the EPA finalized its science-based endangerment finding for heat-trapping emissions, including carbon pollution. The EPA further acted in 2015, when it finalized the Clean Power Plan, the first-ever limits on carbon pollution from power plants.

Case Studies in Obstruction

Most Americans support EPA regulation of carbon pollution, including from power plants. Nonetheless, as evidenced below, fossil fuel and utility interests have stood in the way of EPA action on climate change at each step along the way, and these efforts continue today.

- Peabody Energy denies the scientific consensus on climate change in its attacks on the EPA.
- Southern Company secretly funded an outspoken climate skeptic, while seeking to roll back EPA limits on carbon pollution.
- American Coalition for Clean Coal Electricity has lobbied state attorneys general to oppose EPA limits on carbon pollution.
- American Legislative Exchange Council lobbies state legislators to oppose EPA regulation of carbon pollution on behalf of fossil fuel and utility interests.
- U.S. Chamber of Commerce opposes EPA's science-based finding that heat-trapping emissions and climate change endanger public health, welfare, and the environment.

Now, however, these companies and industry trade groups are increasingly being held accountable for their years of deception and obstructionism. Growing public awareness and concern will further empower efforts to counter their undue influence, and open the door to further progress.

ExxonMobil

Evidence now strongly suggests that ExxonMobil, the world's largest investor-owned producer of oil and natural gas, knew about the potential risks posed by climate change as far back as 1977. Nonetheless, ExxonMobil has spent millions of dollars to fund climate skeptic organizations that oppose the EPA's efforts to act on climate.

ExxonMobil now publicly admits that "the risks of climate change are real and warrant action." And yet the company still opposes EPA action to limit carbon pollution from power plants. Rex Tillerson, CEO of ExxonMobil, disparaged the Clean Power Plan in a 2015 speech before the National Association of Manufacturers. Tillerson claimed to support "comprehensive and science-based cost-benefit analysis" of EPA regulations, but in reality ExxonMobil has funded special interest groups behind misleading reports that artificially inflate the costs and ignore the benefits of the Clean Power Plan. In 2014, ExxonMobil was also named in industry comments calling on the EPA to withdraw its Clean Power Plan proposal.

In 2009, prior to opposing the Clean Power Plan, ExxonMobil joined industry group comments that demanded the EPA withdraw its then-proposed endangerment finding for heat-trapping emissions, including carbon dioxide. The group's comments falsely claimed scientific "support for the effects of climate change on public health and welfare is almost non-existent and engulfed in an extremely high degree of uncertainty."

In 2008, a whistleblower identified lobbying by ExxonMobil as one reason why the administration of President George W. Bush stopped the EPA from going public with an earlier version of the endangerment finding.

ExxonMobil now faces multiple legal investigations for allegedly misleading investors and the public about the risks of climate change. Citizens and shareholders are voicing concerns about ExxonMobil's ongoing funding of special interest groups, such as the American Legislative Exchange Council (ALEC) and the U.S. Chamber of Commerce, that seek to roll back the Clean Power Plan.

Peabody Energy

Peabody Energy, the world's largest investor-owned coal company, has a long and ongoing record of deception on climate change that dates back to the early 1990s. It includes steadfast opposition to EPA regulation of heat-trapping carbon pollution.

Federal courts rejected several Peabody Energy-backed legal challenges aimed at blocking the Clean Power Plan, before the Supreme Court narrowly voted in early 2016 to place implementation of the EPA's final rule on hold until remaining litigation is resolved.

Peabody Energy denied the clear scientific consensus on climate change in its 2014 comments on the EPA's Clean Power Plan proposal. The company's comments claimed that "no science supports the relevant causal links – the connection between changes in GHG [greenhouse gas] levels and any changes in climate." Peabody Energy also funded a misleading 2014 report by Energy Ventures Analysis, which artificially inflated the costs and ignored the benefits of the EPA's proposal.

Before opposing the Clean Power Plan, Peabody Energy challenged the EPA's 2009 endangerment finding for heat-trapping emissions. The company's petition was one of several that, according to the EPA, wrongly "claimed that climate science can't be trusted, and asserted a conspiracy that calls into question the findings of the Intergovernmental Panel on Climate Change, the U.S. National Academy of Sciences, and the U.S. Global Change Research Program." The EPA denied these petitions, having "found no evidence to support these claims."

Earlier, in 2001, then President George W. Bush, under pressure from industry lobbyists, reneged on a campaign pledge to regulate carbon pollution in a letter to members of the US Senate.

"We applaud the announcement this week that the Administration did not support regulation of carbon dioxide as an air pollutant under the Clean Air Act; the position reflects one of our central guiding principals [sic]," wrote Irl Engelhardt, then CEO of Peabody Energy, in a private thank you note to Vice President Dick Cheney that was made public through a Freedom of Information Act request filed by the Natural Resources Defense Council.

A multi-year investigation by the attorney general for the State of New York resulted in a 2015 settlement that found Peabody Energy misled investors and the public about climate change-related financial risks. Peabody Energy has since declared bankruptcy, as the electricity market has shifted away from coal, the largest source of carbon pollution, and towards cleaner sources of electricity.

Southern Company

Southern Company, one of the nation's largest electric utilities, has been at the forefront of disinformation campaigns targeting climate science and solutions since the early 1990s, and remains a staunch opponent of EPA action on climate change.

In 2016, the Supreme Court narrowly voted to place a hold on Clean Power Plan implementation, while the courts consider the merits of legal challenges backed by Southern Company. Internal emails made public by a 2014 New York Times investigation revealed that Southern Company lobbied state attorneys general to urge a federal court to "set aside" the Clean Power Plan proposal. That same year, Southern Company's chief environmental officer called on the EPA to "withdraw its proposed rule."

Southern Company secretly funded the outspoken climate skeptic Willie Soon until 2015, when a high profile investigation forced the utility company to finally sever its ties. Soon's employer, the Smithsonian Institute, also distanced itself from Soon's controversial views, reiterated its own support for the established science on climate change, and launched an ethics review.

Earlier, in 2009, Southern Company endorsed the comments of the Utility Air Regulatory Group, which attacked the science underpinning the EPA's endangerment finding for heat-trapping emissions.

In 2001, an influential lobbyist for Southern Company sent the administration of President George W. Bush a private memo, "Demurring on the issue of whether the CO_2 idea is eco-extremism," and opposing regulation of this heat-trapping emission as a pollutant. Bush, under pressure from industry lobbyists, reneged on a campaign pledge to regulate carbon pollution in a letter to members of the US Senate.

Peer-reviewed academic research has shown that Southern Company could face significant financial risks if the company is held legally liable for the climate change damages resulting from power plants' carbon pollution.

American Coalition for Clean Coal Electricity

The American Coalition for Clean Coal Electricity (ACCCE) serves as a front group for coal and utility interests. It opposes climate action, including the EPA's efforts to limit carbon pollution.

In 2016, the Supreme Court voted narrowly to place a hold on Clean Power Plan implementation, while the courts consider the merits of legal challenges backed by ACCCE.

Internal emails made public by a 2014 New York Times investigation revealed that ACCCE secretly lobbied state attorneys general to urge a federal court to "set aside" the EPA's Clean Power Plan to limit carbon pollution from power plants. ACCCE also funded a series of misleading reports by NERA Economic Consulting, which sought to artificially inflate the costs and ignore the benefits of the Clean Power Plan.

Asked in 2009 if coal-fired plants, the nation's largest single source of heat-trapping carbon pollution, contributed to climate change, a spokesperson for ACCCE refused to say. "I don't know," he told CNN. "I am not a scientist."

That same year, ACCCE claimed to support Congressional action on climate change as an alternative to EPA regulation under the Clean Air Act. But, at the time, ACCCE was a subject of a congressional investigation into fraudulent letters that were sent to members of Congress by an associated public relations firm in an attempt to undermine climate change legislation.

In a leaked 2004 letter to the CEO of Peabody Energy, the Center for Energy and Economic Development, which later became the American Coalition for Clean Coal Electricity (ACCCE), took credit for several state attorneys general joining industry-backed opposition to EPA action on climate change in the federal courts.

Fossil fuel and utility industry support for ACCCE's controversial attacks is on the wane, as evidenced by the group's downsized budget and staff and ongoing corporate exodus. At least two dozen members have departed ACCCE since 2008, such as BHP Billiton, Consol Energy, Consumers Energy, Detroit Edison, Duke Energy, and First Energy. Companies that remain members include Southern Company and bankrupt coal companies, including Alpha Natural Resources and Peabody Energy.

American Legislative Exchange Council (ALEC)

The American Legislative Exchange Council engages with state legislators in secretive meetings sponsored by fossil fuel and utility interests. ALEC is the source of many so-called "model policies" opposing EPA limits on carbon pollution and other clean energy policies.

"The biggest scam of the last 100 years is global warming," one member of ALEC's Private Enterprise Advisory Board said during the group's 2015 annual meeting, at one of the few sessions open to reporters. ALEC's Energy, Natural Resources, and Agriculture Task Force also approved new proposals that would hinder states' ability to comply with the Clean Power Plan. One such ALEC proposal calls for state legislators to expedite use of state funds to back legal challenges to the Clean Power Plan. Sponsors of the annual meeting included the American Coalition for Clean Coal Electricity, Chevron, and ExxonMobil.

Leaked documents from ALEC's 2014 annual meeting revealed another session where Joseph Bast, the president of the Heartland Institute, falsely claimed that "there is no scientific consensus on the human role in climate change." That same year, ALEC approved a resolution that stated, "EPA should not pursue regulation of greenhouse gases," and reportedly agreed to create a "working group" to explore abolishing the EPA as we know it. Internal documents obtained by *The Guardian* also exposed ALEC's plan to recruit state attorneys general to oppose EPA action.

During the George W. Bush administration, ALEC joined the fossil fuel and utility industries' early opposition to EPA action on climate change. In 2007, ALEC called on the EPA not to make an endangerment finding, and claimed there was a "lack of evidence that human-caused emissions of greenhouse gases will 'endanger public health." Several years earlier, in 2003, ALEC criticized efforts by state attorneys general to compel the EPA to act as "frivolous lawsuits… based on inconclusive science and faulty logic." And in 2002, ALEC adopted a resolution that opposed any limits on heat-trapping carbon pollution.

The controversy over ALEC's long and ongoing record of climate deception has helped to spark a mass exodus of more than 100 corporate funders from the group, including fossil fuel and utility companies American Electric Power, BP, and Shell. ExxonMobil and Peabody Energy remain leading members of ALEC's Private Enterprise Advisory Council.

US Chamber of Commerce

The US Chamber of Commerce (US Chamber) claims to represent the interests of the business community, but few companies publicly agree with the group's controversial positions on climate change. Opposing the EPA's efforts to regulate heat-trapping emissions under the Clean Air Act, including the endangerment finding, remains a priority for the US Chamber.

The US Chamber is at the center of lawsuits aimed at blocking EPA action on climate change. Lawyers for the U.S. Chamber Litigation Center filed one of several requests for an immediate stay of the final Clean Power Plan, which the Supreme Court granted in 2016. In 2014, the U.S. Chamber joined ACCCE and Southern Company in soliciting state attorneys general to urge the D.C. Circuit Court to "set aside" the final version of this rule, several months before the EPA had put forth its initial proposal.

The US Chamber has also attempted to use deeply flawed and biased economic analysis that artificially inflates the perceived costs and ignores the benefits of the Clean Power Plan, but its misleading claims have been thoroughly dismantled by media fact checkers and clean energy experts.

A 2012 D.C. Circuit Court decision rejected earlier attempts by the US Chamber and others to roll back the EPA's final endangerment finding for heat-trapping emissions. A few years before, in 2009, the U.S. Chamber called for a "Scopes Monkey Trial of the 21st Century" in response to the EPA's then-proposed endangerment finding. "It would be evolution versus creationism," US Chamber Vice President William Kovacs said at the time. "It will be climate change science on trial."

Internal documents also show that Kovacs represented the U.S. Chamber at a 1999 meeting convened by the American Petroleum Institute, to coordinate the early industry response to calls for the EPA to act on climate change.

The US Chamber's years of obstructionism on climate change have sparked considerable dissent among its corporate membership and local chambers. Major corporations—including several electric utilities—have quit the Chamber over its controversial positions. Current members of the US Chamber include ExxonMobil, Peabody Energy, and Southern Company.

11

State-Level Regulation to Combat Climate Change

Allison Hoppe

Allison Hoppe is a law clerk at the EPA Office of General Counsel. She is a graduate of Cornell University's School of Law.

In this viewpoint, Hoppe provides an analysis of the structural and political dynamics of the US government at the local, state, regional, and federal level. She argues that state regulatory agencies are best positioned to enact effective climate policies. Hoppe asserts that reaching the consensus necessary to implement regulatory action is more likely to be accomplished at the smaller state scale, as political polarization stands in the way of reaching an agreement at the federal level.

C limate change is a global issue that has been gaining awareness on the local, national, and international levels for decades, but thus far the United States has taken very little meaningful governmental action to address the current effects of climate change or to attempt to reduce future impacts. Although there have been some efforts—ranging from purely symbolic to potentially impactful—at all levels of governance to address the causes

"State-Level Regulation as the Ideal Foundation for Action on Climate Change: A Localized Beginning to the Solution of a Global Problem," by Allison C.C. Hoppe, Cornell Law Review, November, 6, 2016. http://scholarship.law.cornell.edu/clr/vol101/iss6/5. This Article is brought to you for free and open access by the Journals at Scholarship@Cornell Law: A Digital Repository. It has been accepted for inclusion in Cornell Law Review by an authorized editor of Scholarship@Cornell Law: A Digital Repository.

and effects of climate change, through response, mitigation or adaptation, so far these have all fallen short of what many scientists believe is necessary to avoid the most severe or irreversible consequences. Because climate change is, by its nature, a broad issue that affects the entire planet, it might seem logical to assume that it primarily requires an international solution. However, the current political climate, both among the international community and within the United States, has made an effective and timely international or national solution almost impossible. Even the significant 2015 Paris Agreement, widely considered an international climate-change law success story, largely lacks binding language and enforcement mechanisms and contains a simple withdrawal clause, leaving the door open for the next U.S. president to withdraw easily. Considering the existing barriers to larger-scale action and absent a major event causing a sudden and dramatic shift in political will, the most effective approach to addressing climate change within the United States is at the state level, through agency regulatory action.

With global average temperatures rising, there has been a correlated increase in the frequency of certain natural disasters, including wildfires, droughts, floods, hurricanes, and others. While no single event can be said to have been caused solely by climate change, numerous scientists have shown that climate change influences various factors that lead to an increased rate of such events occurring. Additionally, sea level rise and ocean acidification is directly related to climate change, and many coastal areas in the United States have begun to experience the effects of the rising oceans. Human, animal and plant life have already been adversely affected by climate change, and these effects will only increase in intensity over time unless serious steps are taken to mitigate the effects of and adapt to climate change. The effects of climate change have already begun to significantly shape national and international politics, result in negative economic impacts, influence international relations, and affect national security and immigration concerns.

Considering the need for governmental action to prevent climate change from becoming more severe and to respond to its current effects, the issue of how advocates of U.S. action on climate change should focus their efforts on inspiring government action is a critically important one. Although a coordinated and concerted effort at all levels of government would clearly be the ideal approach to addressing climate change, the current political reality in the United States minimizes the possibility of a sufficiently significant commitment to curb emissions occurring within the requisite timeframe. Scientists have found that in order to prevent the most catastrophic effects of climate change from becoming nearly inevitable, global average temperatures can increase no more than 2° C beyond 1990 temperatures. Achieving this would necessitate stabilizing atmospheric carbon dioxide concentrations somewhere between 350–400 parts per million and would require an approximately 80% reduction in carbon dioxide emissions below current levels by 2050 for most industrialized countries.

Despite the abundant availability of scientific research expounding the measures that are necessary to prevent or mitigate the effects of climate change, politicians and policymakers—particularly in the United States—have largely failed to act. Unfortunately, it is probable that a major instigating event or crisis will be necessary to spur significant political action. However, in the absence of a shift in political will, one somewhat counterintuitive approach to governmental action could prove the most effective means of addressing climate change in the United States.

This Note argues that the most effective approach to addressing climate change in the current political environment is to focus on state-level regulatory action. Part I of this Note provides the context and brief overview of governmental efforts to address climate change at the state, regional, and federal levels, and in the international context. In Part II, this Note presents arguments against placing the primary focus of governmental efforts at the regional, federal, or international levels and against focusing more on state legislation than on state regulation. Part III advocates for pursuing governmental action on climate change at the state level, particularly through regulation. The Note concludes by highlighting that this argument is made within the context of the current political environment, and emphasizes the importance of U.S. governmental action on climate change at all levels simultaneously whenever possible.

Climate Change Law and Regulation in the United States

State-Level Legislation and Regulation of Climate Change

To date, at least thirty-five states have adopted some method of reducing or capping greenhouse gas emissions within their borders. As of 2008, twenty-six states and the District of Columbia had established renewable portfolio standards for energy suppliers that require a certain percentage of their portfolio to come from renewable power sources. For most of these programs, the percentage required to come from renewable sources increases gradually over time so that energy suppliers have sufficient time to adjust.

The clear leader among the states in terms of action to address climate change is California. The second highest emitter after Texas, California ranks among the "top 20 emitters in the world, including all countries" but, more so than Texas, California has taken significant steps to mitigate its contribution to climate change. In 2006, California passed a landmark climate change law, the California Global Warming Solutions Act, which acknowledged that global warming posed a serious threat to the state and set goals for emission reductions. California also committed to significant water-use reductions in 2009, aiming for a 20% reduction in per capita water use by 2020.

California's state version of the National Environmental Policy Act (NEPA), the California Environmental Quality Act (CEQA) is particularly interesting because its application to climate change has the potential to "force substantive changes in agency practices." This may be the case because CEQA "prohibits an agency from approving a project that will have significant environmental impacts if feasible alternatives or feasible mitigation measures could avoid or substantially lessen those impacts."

One of California's most influential and contentious efforts at addressing greenhouse gas emissions has been spearheaded by the California Air Resources Board (CARB), established in 1967, which "sets air quality standards and regulates vehicular emissions." California ran into trouble when the state enacted a law requiring CARB to establish greenhouse gas emission standards for vehicles and CARB complied by setting standards that would go into effect in 2009. Automakers sued CARB, claiming it was preempting federal authority to set fuel efficiency standards, and the "Environmental Protection Agency [(EPA)] refused to grant California a Clean Air Act waiver, which is needed to adopt state auto emission standards that are stricter than federal limits." It was not until 2009 that the EPA, under President Barack Obama, not only granted California its request for a Clean Air Act waiver but also built upon California's program to develop new federal emission standards.

New York closely follows California as a leader among U.S. states in developing climate change policy and regulation. New York has more stringent laws and regulations regarding environmental impacts of state actions than most other states due to its State Environmental Quality Review (SEQR) requirements. Similar to California's CEQA, New York's SEQR law resembles NEPA, and it requires that all government actors conduct an environmental impact assessment before going forward with almost all state activities, projects, or permits.

[...]

Recently, New York took significant steps toward addressing climate change when it enacted the Community Risk and Resiliency Act in 2014. This act grants certain state agencies significant regulatory authority over climate change adaptation and mitigation measures and requires that all state funds and permits take climate change risks, mitigation, and adaptation into account. New York is the only state in the country with requirements that state funds and permitting processes must all take climate change into account. The enactment of the Community Risk and Resiliency Act was particularly notable because it passed with broad bipartisan support in the wake of recent disasters such as Hurricane Irene in 2011 and Hurricane Sandy in 2012.

In Maryland, what started as a plan for coastal resources expanded and developed to include "human health, agriculture, ecosystems, water resources, and infrastructure." The State of Washington has developed a climate change adaptation plan with numerous focus areas, including: the natural environment, ecosystems, species, habitat, natural resources, infrastructure, communities, human health, and security. Washington, Oregon, and Massachusetts have all implemented regulatory programs that either limit emissions from coal-fired power plants or require that the power plants offset a portion of their emissions. In addition, Massachusetts adopted the Greenhouse Gas Emissions Policy in 2007 that mandates the quantification of greenhouse gas emissions for many state projects and the development of alternatives to the projects that include measures to "avoid, minimize, or mitigate" emissions.

Numerous other states have taken moderate to significant actions toward addressing climate change through mitigation or adaptation, although there are a number of states that have not yet taken any legislative or regulatory steps regarding climate change. However, as a result of the recent Clean Power Plan promulgated under the Environmental Protection Agency's Clean Air Act authority, almost every state will now be required to implement emissions reduction plans. The Clean Power Plan may result in an increase in non-federally mandated state action on climate change as each state evaluates where it can best curb emissions to comply with the plan. However, the Clean Power Plan is currently being challenged in the courts by a coalition of states, corporations, and industry groups, and the case is likely to eventually reach the Supreme Court. Overall, however, the trend among states taking independent action appears to be in the direction of states such as California, New York, and Massachusetts.

[...]

Bigger Is Not Always Better: Why Larger-Scale Attempts at Addressing Climate Change Are Less Effective

The Inefficiencies and Uncertainties of International Action

Political gridlock at the national level is one of the major reasons that the United States has not yet made significant international commitments regarding climate change and curbing greenhouse gas emissions. The attempts at reaching agreement in international climate change talks in recent years have all resulted in failure, in large part due to the fact that developing countries are unwilling to commit to reducing their impact on climate change when the United States and other industrialized countries refuse to commit to more substantial reductions. Developing countries claim that industrialized countries have already gotten their "head start" and should commit to greater cutbacks to reflect the greater period of time spent emitting a higher percentage of pollutants. Until the United States agrees to much more significant reductions in emissions or some other arrangement that reflects the greater impact that the U.S.'s development and current economy has on the climate, any meaningful international agreement is extremely unlikely. While the recent Paris Agreement has largely overcome this particular political obstacle by allowing countries to participate independently using five-year cycles and increasing emissions reductions targets, this agreement remains somewhat precarious because of its largely non-binding nature, the lack of enforcement mechanisms, and the ease with which countries can withdraw.

One of the only earlier international climate change agreements to which the U.S. committed, the United Nations Framework Convention on Climate Change, was only committed to because it contained no legally-binding provisions and instead simply discussed voluntary measures that states could take to address climate change and limit greenhouse gas emissions. This agreement was followed by the 1997 Kyoto Protocol, which the United States signed but never even submitted to the Senate for possible ratification. All efforts at international agreement on binding provisions limiting emissions and addressing climate change have failed to achieve significant commitments, particularly from the United States.

Even significant developments such as the recent climate agreement between the U.S. and China are vague, open-ended, and leave parties with significant room to maneuver. Moreover, many scientists and policymakers view the agreement between the United States and China as achieving only the bare minimum, and argue that both countries, but especially China, should be committing to even more significant reductions in greenhouse gas emissions. While the agreement between the U.S. and China may have helped pave the way for the Paris Agreement, which successfully balanced the interests of developed and developing countries, this agreement remains largely non-binding and has yet to be tested by time, changes in U.S. administrations, or shifts in global politics.

The Improbability of Significant Federal Legislative or Regulatory Action

Despite the fact that the vast majority of the scientific and academic communities recognize the reality of climate change and advocate taking action to mitigate its effects and adapt to its consequences, the political will to take national-level action regarding climate change is lacking. Among the general public, about 67% of Americans believe that global warming is occurring and about 44% of Americans believe that it is caused primarily by human activity.

However, there are distinct partisan divides hidden within these general percentages. Among Democrats or Democrat-leaning Americans, 84% believe that there is "solid evidence the earth is warming" and 64% attribute this to human activity. Within the Republican Party and Republican-leaning Americans, 46% believe climate change is occurring and only 23% think that this is due to human activity. While the contrasting perspectives illustrated by these percentages show that there is a certain ideological divide regarding climate change in the United States, this gap between Democrats and Republicans expands dramatically and disproportionately within Congress. Although necessarily imprecise (some Republican Congress-people have not publicly clarified their views on climate change), one recent estimate found that the proportion of Republican representatives willing to acknowledge that climate change is real is shockingly low at approximately 3%.

The divide in beliefs regarding the validity of climate change between the political parties at the national level is disproportionately wide and has resulted in political gridlock on the issue. Moreover, this current unyielding tension is unlikely to relent in the near future. With the Republicans controlling the House and the Senate at least through the end of 2016, there will almost certainly be no meaningful legislation in the near future regarding climate change absent a significant change in political will.

Additionally, previous efforts at federal action on climate change have resulted in very little positive progress. In fact, Congress has a history of being actively obstructionist and regressive on climate change. In the 1990s, during the buildup to the Kyoto Protocol, the House of Representatives actively prevented spending on any measure that "could be interpreted as paving the way for implementing the Kyoto Protocol." The Senate, in anticipation of the negotiations surrounding the Protocol, passed a resolution stating opposition to any climate change treaty that did not impose obligations on developing nations or that might negatively impact U.S. economic interests.

The efforts at the federal level to stall or prevent action on climate change have not been limited to Congress. During President George W. Bush's terms in office, he attempted to revoke the United States' signature on the Kyoto Protocol even though it was non-binding on the U.S. because it had never been ratified. Although the Bush administration took nominal action on climate change by implementing a policy on greenhouse gas emissions focused on emission intensity, this policy limited certain greenhouse gas emissions while simultaneously allowing for an increase in overall emissions. In fact, members of the Bush administration questioned the science behind climate change and "engaged in a systematic effort to manipulate climate change science and mislead policymakers and the public about the dangers of global warming." The administration achieved this largely by "censor[ing] congressional testimony on the causes and impacts of global warming, control[ling] media access to government climate scientists, and edit[ing] federal scientific reports to inject unwarranted uncertainty into discussions of climate change."

While the recently promulgated Clean Power Plan is a critical and historic step toward reducing greenhouse gas emissions, it faces constant opposition from the Republican majority in the legislature and would almost certainly be overturned under a Republican administration. The plan continues to face challenges in court and some state governors have threatened to refuse to comply, so whether the plan will indeed have its intended effect remains to be seen.

Considering the prevailing attitudes among the congressional majority regarding climate change, the limitations on executive action without congressional support, and the possibility of a climate change denier becoming president, it is extremely unlikely that there will be any significant federal action, particularly legislation, on climate change in the near future.

[…]

Conclusion

Although it may initially appear counterintuitive to advocate approaching a global issue from a more local starting point, the political will requisite to achieving broader national or international policies, laws, or solutions to the issues of climate change is simply not yet existent in the United States or within the international community. Because of the ongoing polarization and reticence of the political actors on both the national and international levels, the best approach to addressing climate change in the United States is to start with state regulatory action.

By serving as the test laboratories and centers of innovation for the federal government and by demonstrating to federal-level politicians that there is political will and economic justification behind local-level climate-change regulatory actions, state agencies are best positioned to incite larger-scale government action on climate change. Additionally, state agencies are equipped with the expertise and information necessary to develop regulations that are specific to the individual state's climate-change adaptation and mitigation needs and strengths. Although federal government action is critical to large-scale efforts to address climate change and plays a significant role in international agreements, state-level regulatory action is the ideal approach in the current political environment to build a strong foundation of U.S. action on climate change from which the other levels of government can build.

Ultimately, if there is any real "solution" to the complex and multifaceted problem of climate change, it is one that will arise out of action taken at all levels of governance. Instead of succumbing to inaction and passively waiting until a global or national approach to addressing climate change is developed, states have the opportunity to start now to play a role in limiting the sources of climate change, preparing for its effects, and putting pressure on actors at all other levels to join them in taking action. Until concerted action on the part of the federal government or the international community is a political possibility, state-level regulatory action provides the best hope of and inspiration for effective U.S. governmental action toward mitigating and adapting to climate change.

12

The Importance of Grassroots Movements in Mobilizing Environmental Action

Petra Bartosiewicz and Marissa Miley

Petra Bartosiewicz is a freelance writer and the recipient of an Alicia Patterson Fellowship, an Open Society Foundation Criminal Justice Fellowship, and a Knight Wallace Fellowship in Journalism. Marissa Miley is the health and environment editor at The GroundTruth Project. *She previously held positions with the Kaiser Family Foundation and GlobalPost.*

This viewpoint examines efforts to mobilize environmental action on the federal level since the 2012 presidential election. The authors suggest that grassroots activism and mobilization will be key factors in the success of these efforts going forward. They assert that attempts to address climate change have been ineffective because of an unwillingness to address market capitalist forces , as well as a focus on experts and insiders rather than the general public in environmental advocacy. A more radical and populist grassroots movement will be necessary for environmental action.

[…]

The 2012 presidential campaign featured a slate of Republican candidates who labeled climate change as "manufactured science," a "hoax," and "all one contrived phony mess." The party's eventual nominee, former Massachusetts governor Mitt Romney,

"The Too Polite Revolution," by Petra Bartosiewicz and Marissa Miley, National Academy of Sciences, January 2013. Reprinted by permission of the authors.

backpedaled from a June 2011 statement that "it's important for us to reduce our emissions of pollutants and greenhouse gases." Several months later, he declared, "We don't know what's causing climate change on this planet, and the idea of spending trillions and trillions of dollars to try to reduce CO_2 emissions is not the right course for us." Obama, facing a tough reelection campaign, shelved plans to tighten Bush-era ozone standards and instead advocated for "the importance of reducing regulatory burdens and regulatory uncertainty, particularly as our economy continues to recover." In contrast to the 2008 presidential campaign, which featured two nominees who both openly declared their support for placing a cap on carbon emissions, not a single mention of climate change was made by either Obama or Romney during their three debates. In his victory speech on election night, Obama said he wanted to build an America that "isn't threatened by the destructive power of a warming planet," but he focused most of his remarks on creating new jobs. Exit polls, meanwhile, showed that voters' concerns about the economy topped their other concerns by a wide margin.

The year 2012 is now on record as the hottest year in the United States, but Congress is by all accounts further away from passing climate change legislation than it was when President Obama was elected in 2008. As we have documented in this report, there were significant external factors that contributed to this lost opportunity. Individuals from all sides of the issue with whom we spoke, particularly members of the green groups, believe the outcome might have been different had the economy been stronger, had Congress been less partisan, had climate gone before health care in the Senate, and had President Obama taken on more of a leadership role during crucial moments in the legislative process. "Hardly any major environmental legislation has been passed in bad economic times," said Nikki Roy. "What really finally killed it for us was the president not taking the lead on the legislative effort."

But the green groups also made a number of strategic assumptions that ended up hurting them in their pursuit of climate policy. They were mistaken in their belief that brokering a deal with traditional adversaries through USCAP would automatically garner support from congressional leaders, particularly the midwestern Democrats and Republicans whose lack of support proved so crucial. Moreover, despite having more money than ever before to fund their campaign, the green groups remained vastly outspent by their opposition and did not have enough influence with individual congressional leaders to win with an overwhelmingly inside game strategy. The GOP's sharp rightward shift with the rise of the Tea Party in 2009 only made this strategy more difficult to execute. A groundswell of public support may not have been enough to turn the tide, but even so, the green groups believed the public would rally around the cap- and-trade bill without any substantial investment in cultivating such a broad base of support.

Additionally, there were factors that were, to some degree, within the green groups' control. They could have been better prepared for the Senate battle after the narrow House victory in June 2009, and they could have more vigorously pressured the White House to support the bill. They also could have built a more robust coalition of non-environmental allies to sharply articulate the green jobs argument that the administration seemed eager to promote. President Obama's top priority, before he was even sworn into office, was to prevent the economy from entering into free fall. Members of his administration described to us the need for the very kind of green jobs effort that was lacking in the cap-and-trade legislative campaign. The green groups may not have been the best messengers for this position, but they could have leveraged stronger partnerships with labor groups early on.

With the worsening economy, one of the Obama administration's chief concerns, the green groups could also have sought a scaled-down version of cap and trade in the form of a utility-only bill, which Rahm Emanuel reportedly supported. EDF's Fred Krupp told us, however, that passing such a scaled-down bill would have been nearly as difficult as passing economy-wide carbon legislation. "At the time, there was nobody in the U.S. who thought we could keep the Democrats on a utility-only bill," he said.

At the same time, critics of the big greens and in particular, the USCAP coalition, argue that by bringing American corporations to the table from the start, the environmental community negotiated away far too much, and that USCAP itself was an excessive compromise that came too early in the legislative game. Staffers on Capitol Hill told us that the green groups often "confuse access with influence." The focus of the lobbying effort was cap and trade, they said, but once the environmental groups achieved the goal of getting legislation on the table, they lost much of their ability to influence the shape that legislation would take.

Despite the failure of cap and trade to pass in the Senate in this most recent effort, leaders of many green groups told us that enacting federal carbon legislation remains imperative. And yet, the defeat in 2010 was so profound that it's unclear when another attempt can be made. In the months leading up to the 2012 presidential election, there was no evidence that the green groups were mounting the kind of climate legislation campaign they were preparing to unveil four years earlier. There was no relaunch of USCAP, no collaborative marshaling of resources around climate legislation, and no clear picture for what such a climate policy might look like. Fred Krupp, an early and the most steadfast proponent of cap and trade, told us, "We're open to any idea."

Other members of the environmental community do not believe an emissions cap is the right policy to push first. Michael Shellenberger and Ted Nordhaus, founders of the Breakthrough Institute, a public policy think tank, argue that the emphasis instead should be on lowering the cost of clean energy. Public investment in clean energy technology research and development will drive down costs and spur innovation, they say, citing the military's procurement of new defense technology as a model. In their view, such investment will also reduce carbon emissions as the nation moves toward cleaner (and cheaper) energy. Wind, solar, and nuclear technologies "have a long way to go" if they are to adequately replace fossil fuels, Shellenberger and Nordhaus wrote in a February 2012 article for Yale's *e360*. "But the key to getting there won't be more talk of caps and carbon prices."

The primarily West Coast funders that backed cap and trade also seem to be at an impasse around climate. Unlike in 2007, when the publication of "Design to Win" helped catalyze unprecedented levels of funding for climate change solutions in the United States, there is no clear vision for what policies should be pursued going forward. The former head of ClimateWorks, Hal Harvey, who was so influential in shaping the cap- and-trade campaign, resigned from the organization in December 2011, and Paul Brest, president of the Hewlett Foundation, has since retired. In an early 2012 letter circulated to Hewlett trustees, a number of environmental organizations, such as Friends of the Earth and the Rainforest Action Network, called for the large foundation to find a new leader who would depart from the current strategy in which "strategic philanthropy too often favors a linear, excessively technocratic view of social change." "What we're seeing now is certainly a retrenchment to the states," said Matthew Lewis, former director of communications at ClimateWorks. "There is certainly a robust discussion going on about how you build real and enduring political power, and I'm pretty sure it's safe to say you don't do that in Washington, D.C."

While much of the green groups' postmortem discussion around the failure to pass climate legislation has focused on how they might win next time, there are signs that the groups are beginning to engage and mobilize the grassroots. An article in the *New York Times* last year quoted Maggie Fox, head of the Alliance for Climate Protection (now renamed the Climate Reality Project) as saying that in the run-up to the presidential election, the group had steered away from big television ad buys and was instead refocusing its efforts on social media, training, and organizing. "Whatever we would spend, it would just be washed away in this sea of fossil fuel money," Fox said. Beginning in 2011, the green groups also organized successfully in defense of the EPA's authority to regulate greenhouse gases and other air pollutants by leveraging partnerships with health and advocacy groups such as the American Lung Association and the League of Women Voters. In August 2011, they launched a national ad campaign called "Clean Air Promise" with a focus on protecting the health of children and families from toxic air pollution, which can cause asthma, among other illnesses. In this sense, the green groups are returning to the arena in which they have enjoyed arguably their greatest historic successes—litigation rooted in a concern for public health—and they are rallying precisely the broad support of traditional allies that might have made a difference in the climate campaign. The green groups coordinated their strategy, directing resources to targeted state advertising and public outreach. The environmental community achieved a significant victory when, in December 2011, the EPA issued a ruling that, for the first time ever, required U.S. power plants to limit emissions of mercury and other toxic pollutants. In this case, an unprecedented 900,000 Americans submitted public comments to the EPA in support of the standard.

On the state level, a victory on carbon emissions reductions in California in November 2010 showed the effectiveness of grassroots engagement. Activists in California rallied nearly six million voters to defeat Proposition 23, a legislative effort bankrolled by out-of-state oil companies and the Koch brothers to reverse AB 32, which set state standards for carbon emission reductions. Grassroots organization, rather than insider lobbying, was key to the victory: more than 130 community-based organizations formed an alliance called Communities United Against the Dirty Energy Proposition. The coalition featured a broad swath of ethnic, environmental, health, religious, and social justice groups along with clean energy advocates and was bolstered by celebrities and more than three thousand volunteers. The campaign reached over two million people, conducting more than 250,000 one-on-one conversations by going door-to-door and making phone calls. It also sent out direct mailings in English, Spanish, and Chinese, placed advertising in ethnic media, and organized get-out-the-vote rallies. The ballot initiative's defeat was aided, too, by the strength of the clean energy sector in California, which has made nearly $9 billion in new investment since the passage of AB 32 in 2006.cxxviii The "No on Prop. 23" campaign was backed by more than $30 million from California venture capitalists, clean tech companies, and environmental groups and outspent its opposition nearly three-to-one.

Another significant grassroots effort, this time at the national level, came in 2011 with the public campaign to halt the controversial expansion of the Keystone XL pipeline. Opponents of the pipeline, which would transport heavy crude oil from western Canadian tar sands to refineries in Texas and Oklahoma via Kansas and Nebraska, argued that extracting and transporting the oil risks environmental contamination through leaks and spills, particularly when the route cuts across the largest aquifer in the United States. While the pipeline's expansion was foremost an issue affecting Canada and a handful of states in the United States, environmentalists saw it as a move toward the exploration of dirtier energy—the Canadian tar sands are the second-largest reserve of carbon in the world. The development of the tar sands, said NASA's climatologist Jim Hansen, means "essentially game over" for the climate. To fight the pipeline's expansion, Hansen teamed up with longtime environmental activist Bill McKibben and other activists, calling in June 2011 for "civil disobedience" in the form of a peaceful protest at the White House. That summer, more than 1,200 people, including Hansen and McKibben, were arrested. When President Obama signaled that he would approve the controversial project, environmental activists rallied some 12,000 supporters to encircle the White House in protest in November. Their efforts got the president's attention. Obama announced he would take another year to review the proposed pipeline. In January 2012, when Republicans in Congress voted to expedite the review, Obama rejected the tactic largely on the basis that concerns about the environmental impact of the pipeline could not be thoroughly analyzed in such a short period of time. As of his reelection in November 2012, Obama had yet to make a final decision on the pipeline, though many observers believe he will ultimately approve the project with a modified route.

Most of the green groups we spoke with understood that any future national climate campaign will need to unite the big green groups with their partners at the local and state levels. When New York, Chicago, San Francisco, and other cities created climate action plans of their own and joined global initiatives for city-level climate mitigation, funders and organizations also took steps to mobilize locally. In July 2011, for example, Bloomberg Philanthropies partnered with the Sierra Club in a $50 million expansion of the group's "Beyond Coal" campaign to shut down coal plants across the country. This effort resulted in 54 coal plants being retired or scheduled for retirement in 2012 alone.

The greens groups also say they understand the need to harness grassroots support. Going forward, it will be critical to get "Americans demanding policy," Fred Krupp told us. But it remains unclear whether the big greens will be able to build this mass demand for a national climate policy, or even whether they will decide it is in their interest to do so. The most visible grassroots mobilization these days is being spearheaded not by organizations like EDF or NRDC, but by groups like Bill McKibben's 350.org, which has successfully mobilized students from more than 190 colleges and universities in a nationwide fossil fuel divestment campaign. "We've got now to put them on the defensive," McKibben recently told Democracy Now!, referring to the fossil fuel companies. "That's what the fight is about. And that's why it's good news that this has suddenly turned into the largest student movement in a very long time." Such a mobilization may be more critical in the coming four years; while President Obama was elected in 2008 with a strong mandate and both the House and Senate were under Democratic control, his reelection in 2012 was accompanied by a divided Congress, making the passage of large-scale legislation more difficult.

"Democratic mobilization becomes the norm when would-be leaders can achieve power and influence only by drawing others into movements, associations, and political battles," Harvard sociologist Theda Skocpol writes in *Diminished Democracy*, her study of civic engagement in American life. This incentive to mobilize was largely absent in the green groups' campaign for climate legislation. Their fundamental assumption was that success lay in negotiating with industry and lawmakers directly, and not in building grassroots support. This reasoning is, of course, not without some merit. A real transformation has taken place in the civic landscape over the past four decades, Skocpol notes, from the days when politicians won office in closely fought, high-turnout elections, and American civic life was characterized by participation in far more local and community-based groups. The focus today on Washington-based advocacy and lobbying is reflected in the expansion of congressional staffers who serve as the primary conduit to elected officials—the number of these staffers has risen from 6,255 in 1960, to 10,739 in 1970, to about 20,000 in 1990. By 2000 the number was 24,000.

The composition of the national green groups today—with their professional staffs and their Washington focus, reflects this shift. But given that the green groups are likely to remain vastly outspent by industry lobby groups that oppose their efforts, future campaigns will run into the same obstacles as in this most recent push for climate legislation. Tapping into the grassroots base and learning how to mobilize the public may be the only way to balance the scales. It was, after all, the rise in the public's environmental consciousness in the 1960s that led to the first Earth Day in 1970 and gave a mandate and a constituency to EDF, NRDC, and the Sierra Club, which then leveraged this energy to push for reforms.

Whatever policy approach is embraced, however, the path to meaningful action will require a fundamental paradigm shift. Climate is the defining issue of our generation. Yet it has not been dealt with directly in the U.S. because to solve this problem requires confronting market capitalist forces that are considered fundamental to the American way of life. As writer Naomi Klein astutely points out in her essay "Capitalism vs. Climate," in The Nation, what climate deniers understand (and green groups don't) is that lowering global carbon emissions to safe levels will be achieved "only by radically reordering our economic and political systems in ways antithetical to their 'free market' belief system." In this sense, writes Klein, the climate deniers have a firmer grasp of the high stakes at the core of the climate debate than "professional environmentalists" who "paint a picture of global warming Armageddon, then assure us that we can avert catastrophe by buying 'green' products and creating clever markets in pollution."

In 1995 Mark Dowie observed in Losing Ground that for too long mainstream environmental advocacy in the U.S. has taken the form of a "polite revolution," one that has been marked from the start by "polite activism" that favors an elitist and insider approach rather than aggressive grassroots and coalitional forms of activism. The failure of the legislative effort during President Obama's first term is perhaps the most definitive evidence to date that climate change will not be resolved through politesse.

13

A Cultural Change Is Necessary to Fight Climate Change

Carol Gould

Carol Gould is a professor of philosophy at Hunter College. She is the editor of the Journal of Social Philosophy *and the author of* Rethinking Democracy: Freedom and Social Cooperation in Politics, Economy, and Society, *among many other publications.*

In this viewpoint, Carol Gould argues that in order to make real progress on climate policies, we first need to undergo a cultural change. She asserts that we must fundamentally change the way that we think about the relationship between the environment and the economy, acknowledging that we cannot continue to favor individual consumerism and materialism—fundamental American values—while effectively combatting climate change. However, she argues that both the climate crisis and the American democratic crisis are rooted in economic inequality, with wealthy individuals and corporations having a disproportionate say in politics and environmental regulation. By addressing the issue of inequality we can tackle both issues.

W hat more would be needed to mitigate dangerous climate change, as well as to adapt to it where necessary? To begin to answer these questions, we would require a solid diagnosis of the

"Beyond the Dual Crisis: From Climate Change to Democratic Change," by Carol Gould was originally published in The Center for Humans & Nature's online journal minding nature, January, 2016, Vol.9 No.1. humansandnature.org.

causes of the present climate crisis. We would need to understand why countries and people worldwide have not yet been able to rise to the challenge of addressing and dealing with the monumental climatic changes that threaten human existence and flourishing on the planet (and that threaten other species as well). In order to arrive at this explanation, and on this basis offer effective policy proposals, I suggest we have to look not only at the climate crisis but also at the democracy crisis.

I want to propose that progress in curbing climate change to proceed concomitantly with transformations in democracy. Indeed, these two crises—of climate and democracy—are supplemented with a third and long-standing one concerning global justice, including pervasive inequality and world poverty. It might even be suggested that we need to bring in a further contemporary crisis—that of global capitalism. This article will investigate the way climate intersects with these other forces and factors— inequality, capitalism, and especially democracy—and will make a few suggestions for a path ahead to address these various crises.

The approach taken here recognizes an important role for what has been called *structural injustice*—in other words, the way institutions, whether political, economic, or social, function to produce and perpetuate forms of human oppression and climatic harm, even if the individuals functioning within these institutions may be well meaning and not specifically intending these negative modes or effects. From this perspective, the oft-cited reliance on individuals as consumers making changes in their attitude or even their behavior—in which they would dramatically lower their own contributions to emissions—can be seen to be inadequate to the task of bringing about fundamental change in planetary outcomes.

A substantial number of theorists have suggested that taking a different attitude toward the natural world is the key factor to deal with climate change—for example, an attitude modeled on indigenous beliefs about the land, or else a spiritual view that emphasizes the interdependence of the natural or biotic world. I want to dispute such claims. If the problem is largely structural, then even though such new or reclaimed attitudes or perspectives may be valuable, they do not deal with the root causes of the climate crisis (or the democracy crisis, as we shall see).

Moreover, I would be highly reluctant to endorse one single attitude or perspective on nature that everyone would be expected to adopt. I will myself propose that we do indeed need to renounce views of human dominance over nature. But the attitude that replaces it can be based on a wide range of theoretical perspectives or approaches, all of which could support a practical attitude to the natural world in which we recognize and act on the recognition that we are an integral part of nature and dependent on it. This recognition does not require abandoning the importance of human goals or intentions and indeed the value of the development of human capacities—both individual and collective—over time. But we need to see humans and their activity as both a part of nature and as interdependent with the natural environment. Social construction of the natural world will necessarily continue—in which we interpret nature and create artifacts through our practical activity—but we need to more clearly understand the way that nature both constrains and enables human ends and processes and merits respect as well.

In order to elaborate these broad themes in this short article, we can begin with the concrete analysis of the crises of climate and democracy and of their root cause(s), move to a brief critique of existing proposals for dealing with them, and conclude with a few suggestions for moving ahead in regard to both domains, at the point of their intersection. Needless to say, both the explanation and the proposals will rely on the ideas of many others, but I believe that the account here brings together the various factors in an original and distinctive way.

Crises in Climate and Democracy—Their Intersection and Their Common Root

The readers of *Minding Nature* are all too familiar with the climate crisis. Suffice it to say that if present emissions rates continue, scientists predict the melting of the polar ice caps, the disappearance of the glaciers (along with the water they supply) including the Greenland ice sheet, the thawing of the permafrost and the potential vast methane release, the rise of sea levels with accompanying inundation of island nations and flooding in coastal cities around the world, the salinization of the oceans, increasingly severe weather disturbances, more widespread droughts, deep problems for agriculture in various regions, and more. These problems are attributed to the increasing concentration of greenhouse gases in the atmosphere, including carbon dioxide, methane, and nitrous oxide. Moreover, carbon in the atmosphere accumulates over time and will apparently take centuries to dissipate, so that the emissions problem becomes more and more acute, even if there are successful efforts to limit emissions. The destruction of tropical rainforests also plays a significant role both in carbon release and in the elimination of valuable carbon sinks. Indeed, the entire process—if unchecked—can be expected to manifest a transformation of quantity into quality—that is, the arrival of a so-called tipping point, leading to climate chaos, with runaway warming, profound degradation in weather, and other dire, uncontrollable consequences.

The democracy crisis at first glance seems altogether different, and it, too, is well known. It involves the hollowing out of real democracy or rule by the people. Instead, corporations and wealthy individuals exert major influence over both elections and public policy. In the United States especially, the role of virtually unlimited campaign donations by the superrich, including by corporations now regarded as "persons" in virtue of the *Citizens United* Supreme Court decision, exacerbates the problems that arise from the distortion of legislation and representation by means of pervasive lobbying by powerful economic interests. Democracy has been reduced at best to "spectatorship," in which citizens can only observe processes over which they have no control, replacing the core democratic modes of active participation in government, which theorists—from John Dewey to the present—have argued are essential to democracy's flourishing.

At the international level as well, the institutions of global governance, including the World Trade Organization, the International Monetary Fund, and even the World Bank, display a "democratic deficit." While these institutions have significant influence over the livelihoods and work conditions of people around the world who are affected by their policies, these people themselves have no opportunities to provide input into these powerful institutions. Instead, these agencies are controlled by large states that often act in the interest of the big corporations within them. Internationally, too, some states lack democracy altogether, including among them major global actors like China.

The two crises—climate and democracy—are directly interrelated by the fact that the kind of regulation and legislation that are called for to address climate change are rendered very difficult by lobbying and campaign contributions that themselves weaken democracy. Among the major players in such lobbying and donations are the fossil fuel industry and the wealthy individuals who run it. On the international stage as well, given the power of large emitting states and corporations on the global governance institutions, it is no surprise that few actions are taken to limit emissions or to offer major support for alternative energy development. Meanwhile, older authoritarian regimes (e.g., China) most often do not address the demands of their own citizens for more livable cities with breathable air.

We can observe, too, that climate change reciprocally exacerbates the problems for democracy. This is evident in the "security crisis" it engenders, bringing increased potential for conflicts between states and regions (whether within or across states). New forms of violent conflict have themselves been attributed in part to climate change—for example, the drought that aggravated the situation in Syria, which can be expected to intensify with the worsening of the climate crisis. Likewise, the refugee crisis that challenges European democracies at this moment is in part caused by climate change, and it is expected to vastly increase and deepen with the displacement of millions from coastal cities in future years. Other forms of human security are threatened as well, especially food security. And if governments and global governance institutions continue to be hobbled by their deference to fossil fuel corporate interests, they are unlikely to take the steps needed to deal with the climate crisis. Further, it is even possible that the rise to prominence of these security issues will lead to an abandonment of democracy itself in favor of authoritarian "solutions." And where democracy still maintains its hold in liberal democratic states, the emphasis on security measures that are seen as required to manage climate change threatens to undercut our commitments to the basic liberties essential for democracy, such as freedom of expression and association.

But there is also, I suggest, a deep interrelation between the two crises under consideration here in a different sense: they can be seen as sharing in large measure the same root cause, a point too often unnoticed or disregarded in analyses of these crises and what to do about them. This observation will allow us to bring in the additional dimension noted at the outset—namely, the issues of deep inequality, global poverty, and injustice that exacerbate the other effects of climate change, producing especially harsh outcomes for developing countries and disadvantaged peoples. Injustice and inequality likewise intensify the democracy crisis, both nationally and internationally, by depriving people of effective voice in the process. In addition, they work against the capacity of democracies to regulate climate change because the affluent are currently much better able to avoid or mitigate its impacts. Moreover, with the deference afforded large corporate interests and wealthy donors, democratic states and global governance institutions alike have fewer incentives to support regulations on emissions or to promote renewable fuels.

An emphasis on structural injustice leads us to focus on the ways in which capitalism as a system functions to produce climate change. Indeed, the consequences it regularly produces for the environment are aggravated by capitalism's own present crisis. Even without extensive political economic analysis, it is evident that the capitalist system depends for its functioning on both competition and growth (at the macro-level of national and international economies, as well as at the micro-level of firms). For the most part, corporations tend to eschew regulation or limitation in the interest of greater profits and capital accumulation. This profit-seeking activity is not in the first place a matter of attitude—say, of greed—but rather a basic mode of functioning of the system. Given the competitive environment (again, at both the macro- and micro-levels), corporate executives and managers see themselves as having no choice but to follow the logic of growth. Moreover, the need for increasing sales leads to an intense emphasis on promoting consumption, and even involves what has been called "the creation of new needs" for consumers, through advertising and other means. Indeed, efforts are made to turn nearly everything into a commodity to be bought and sold, including land and other aspects of the natural world.

In this situation, regulations in the interest of ecological sustainability necessarily come from outside the economy, and are most often viewed as an imposition of constraints on markets. Because of the power of corporate interests, intensified by competition from new corporations in emerging markets in the context of globalization, democratic governments have tended to resist putting in place the necessary environmental (or social) regulations. They most often refuse to impose carbon taxes or to provide serious incentives for the development of renewable fuels. The emphasis on growth and on competition among national economies, combined with the weakening of democracy within these states, in turn contributes to the increased power of corporate lobbies—including especially those of fossil fuel industries—and allows large corporations to flourish at the expense of the meeting of human (and non-human) needs.

We can add that this profit-oriented system operates in a way that generates inequality, as well as a certain measure of exploitation, given the divergent interests of owners/managers and workers/consumers within it. At the global level, inequalities emerge between developed and developing states, as well as within each of these. Given the centrality of competition, cooperative modes of social relationship are devalued within economic or political life. All of this in turn impacts on our dealings with global warming. Well-off individuals and firms can more easily protect themselves against its effects, and their disproportionate influence on politics leads to a lack of political or legislative action to address it. Disadvantaged people and entire countries are left to deal with adapting to climate change practically alone (despite the recent meager and non-binding commitments to international aid included in the Paris Agreement).

From this structural perspective, the contemporary emphasis on individual consumerism and acquisitiveness in the developed countries can be seen as a consequence of the operation of capitalist institutions, rather than as a cause of it. Likewise, the unlimited use (and using up) of the Earth's resources, and the emphasis on extraction without end, are largely driven by an economic system oriented to corporate profit. Of course, none of this is to deny the strengths of this system in producing goods for large numbers of people, as well as the power of economic and technological globalization to increase the scope of interchange and communication across borders. But I believe that if we are to make a fundamental transformation in regard to climate change, we need to confront directly the deep problems with the existing system, especially as they impact both nature and democracy, and attempt to work toward some new directions.

[...]

Organizations to Contact

The editors have compiled the following list of organizations concerned with the issues debated in this book. The descriptions are derived from materials provided by the organizations. All have publications or information available for interested readers. The list was compiled on the date of publication of the present volume; the information provided here may change. Be aware that many organizations take several weeks or longer to respond to inquiries, so allow as much time as possible.

American Association for the Advancement of Science (AAAS)
1200 New York Ave NW
Washington, DC 20005
phone: (202) 326-6400
website: www.aaas.org

The AAAS seeks to "advance science, engineering, and innovation throughout the world for the benefit of all people." It is the world's largest multidisciplinary scientific society and a leading publisher of cutting-edge research.

Environmental Defense Fund (EDF)
1875 Connecticut Ave, NW, Suite 600
Washington, DC 20009
phone: (800) 684-3322
website: www.edf.org
The Environmental Defense Fund (EDF) is a United States-based nonprofit environmental advocacy group. The group is known for its work on issues including global warming, ecosystem restoration, oceans, and human health, and advocates using sound science, economics, and law to find environmental solutions that work.

Intergovernmental Panel on Climate Change (IPCC)
C/O World Meteorological Organization
7bis Avenue de la Paix
C.P. 2300
CH- 1211 Geneva 2, Switzerland
phone: +41-22-730-8208/54/84
email: IPCC-Sec@wmo.int
website: www.ipcc.ch

The Intergovernmental Panel on Climate Change (IPCC) is the international body for assessing the science related to climate change. The IPCC was established in 1988 by the World Meteorological Organization (WMO) and United Nations Environment Programme (UNEP) to provide policymakers with regular assessments of the scientific basis of climate change, its impacts and future risks, and options for adaptation and mitigation.

National Science Foundation (NSF)
2415 Eisenhower Avenue
Alexandria, Virginia 22314
phone: (703) 292-5111
email: info@nsf.gov
website: www.nsf.gov

The National Science Foundation (NSF) is an independent federal agency created by Congress in 1950 "to promote the progress of science; to advance the national health, prosperity, and welfare; to secure the national defense."

The Science Coalition
PO Box 65694
Washington, DC 20036
email: sciencecoalition@hudsonlake.com
website: www.sciencecoalition.org

Established in 1994, the Science Coalition is a nonprofit, nonpartisan organization of more than 50 of the nation's leading public and private research universities. It is dedicated to sustaining the federal government's investment in basic scientific research as a means to stimulate the economy, spur innovation, and drive America's global competitiveness.

Union of Concerned Scientists
2 Brattle Sq.
Cambridge, MA 02138
phone: (617) 547-5552
website: www.ucsusa.org

The Union of Concerned Scientists puts rigorous, independent science to work to solve our planet's most pressing problems. Joining with people across the country, they combine technical analysis and effective advocacy to create innovative, practical solutions for a healthy, safe, and sustainable future.

United States Environmental Protection Agency (EPA)
Environmental Protection Agency
1200 Pennsylvania Avenue, NW
Washington, DC 20460
phone: (202) 564-4700
email: www.epa.gov

The United States Environmental Protection Agency (EPA) is an agency of the federal government that was created for the purpose of protecting human health and the environment by writing and enforcing regulations based on laws passed by Congress.

Bibliography

Books

Stuart Altman and David Shactman. *Power, Politics, and Universal Health Care.* Amherst, NY: Prometheus Books, 2011.

Rachel Carson. *Silent Spring.* New York, NY: First Mariner Books, 2002 (1962 orig).

Al Gore. *An Inconvenient Truth.* New York, NY: Rodale Books, 2006.

Sam Harris. *The Moral Landscape: How Science Can Determine Human Values.* New York, NY: Free Press, 2010.

Andrew J. Hoffman. *How Culture Shapes the Climate Change Debate.* Palo Alto, CA: Stanford University Press, 2015.

Naomi Klein. *This Changes Everything: Capitalism vs. The Climate.* New York, NY: Simon & Schuster, 2014.

Dave Levitan. *Not a Scientist: How Politicians Mistake, Misrepresent, and Utterly Mangle Science.* New York, NY: W.W. Norton & Company, 2017.

Chris Mooney. *The Republican War on Science.* Cambridge, MA: Basic Books, 2005.

Chris Mooney. *Unscientific America: How Scientific Illiteracy Threatens Our Future.* New York, NY: Basic Books, 2009.

Marion Nestle. *Food Politics: How the Food Industry Influences Nutrition and Health.* Berkeley, CA: University of California Press, 2002.

Tom Nichols. *The Death of Expertise: The Campaign Against Established Knowledge and Why It Matters.* New York, NY: Oxford University Press, 2017.

William D. Nordhaus. *The Climate Casino: Risk, Uncertainty, and Economics for a Warming World.* New Haven, CT: Yale University Press, 2013.

Bill Nye. *Unstoppable: Harnessing Science to Change the World.* New York, NY: St. Martin's Griffin, 2015.

Naomi Oreskes and Erik M. Conway. *Merchants of Doubt: How a Handful of Scientists Obscured the Truth on Issues from Tobacco Smoke to Global Warming.* New York, NY: Bloomsbury Press, 2010.

Roger Pielke. *The Climate Fix: What Scientists and Politicians Won't Tell You About Global Warming.* New York, NY: Basic Books, 2010.

Steven Pinker. *Enlightenment Now: The Case for Reason, Science, Humanism, and Progress.* New York, NY: Viking Books, 2018.

Carl Sagan. *The Demon-Haunted World: Science as a Candle in the Dark.* New York, NY: Ballantine Books, 1996.

Periodicals and Internet Sources

John Abraham. "Reflections on the Politics of Climate Change," *Guardian*, June 2, 2017. https://www.theguardian.com/environment/climate-consensus-97-per-cent/2017/jun/02/reflections-on-the-politics-of-climate-change

Frank Bruni. "Too Much Prayer In Politics: Republicans, the Religious Right, and Evolution," *New York Times*, February 14, 2015. https://www.nytimes.com/2015/02/15/opinion/sunday/frank-bruni-republicans-the-religious-right-and-evolution.html

Coral Davenport and Eric Lipton. "How G.O.P. Leaders Came to View Climate Change as Fake Science," *New York Times*, June 3, 2017. https://www.nytimes.com/2017/06/03/us/politics/republican-leaders-climate-change.html?_r=0

Louis A. Del Monte. "Politics in Science," *Huffington Post*, October 29, 2017. https://www.huffingtonpost.com/entry/ politics-in-science_us_59f511fae4b05f0ade1b57cb

Mischa Fisher. "The Republican Party Isn't Really the Anti-Science Party," *Atlantic*, November 11, 2013. https://www. theatlantic.com/politics/archive/2013/11/the-republican-party-isnt-really-the-anti-science-party/281219/

Stephen Fleischfresser. "The more people know about climate change and evolution, the more they disagree," *Cosmos Magazine*, August 25, 2017. https://cosmosmagazine.com/ social-sciences/the-more-people-know-about-climate-change-and-evolution-the-more-they-disagree

Cary Funk. "Democrats far more supportive than Republicans of federal spending for scientific research," Pew Research Center, May 1, 2017. http://www.pewresearch.org/fact-tank/2017/05/01/democrats-far-more-supportive-than-republicans-of-federal-spending-for-scientific-research/

Cary Funk and Lee Rainie. "Americans, Politics, and Science Issues," Pew Research Center, July 1, 2015. http://www. pewinternet.org/2015/07/01/americans-politics-and-science-issues/

Elizabeth Lopatto. "Yes, Science is Political," *Verge*, April 21, 2017. https://www.theverge.com/2017/1/19/14258474/ trump-inauguration-science-politics-climate-change-vaccines

Chris Mooney. "A new battle over politics and science could be brewing. And scientists are ready for it," *Washington Post*, January 31, 2017. https://www.washingtonpost.com/news/ energy-environment/wp/2017/01/31/a-new-battle-over-politics-and-science-could-be-coming-and-scientists-are-ready-for-it/?utm_term=.6429e7618289

Simon Oxenham. "Why Do Most American Conservatives Still Refuse to Believe in Climate Change?" *Big Think*, http://

bigthink.com/neurobonkers/why-do-most-american-conservatives-still-refuse-to-believe-in-climate-change

Elisabeth Pain. "How Scientists Can Influence Policy," *Science Magazine*, February 16, 2014. http://www.sciencemag.org/careers/2014/02/how-scientists-can-influence-policy

William Pierce. "The Role of Science and Politics in Public Policy Decision Making," *Huffington Post*, August 3, 2016. https://www.huffingtonpost.com/william-pierce/the-role-of-science-and-p_b_1734920.html

Steven Pinker and Leon Wieseltier. "Science vs. the Humanities, Round III," *New Republic*, September 26, 2013. https://newrepublic.com/article/114754/steven-pinker-leon-wieseltier-debate-science-vs-humanities

Peter J. Richerson. "What are the roles of scientists in policy-making?" The Evolution Institute, January 14, 2016. https://evolution-institute.org/focus-article/what-are-the-roles-of-scientists-in-policy-making/

Justin Worland. "Climate Change Used to Be a Bipartisan Issue. Here's What Changed," *Time Magazine*, July 27, 2017. http://time.com/4874888/climate-change-politics-history/

Index